The Happy Empath's Workbook

HANDS-ON ACTIVITIES, WORKSHEETS AND STRATEGIES
FOR CREATING A JOYOUS AND FULL LIFE

Stephanie Jameson

ULYSSES PRESS

Published in the United States by:
Ulysses Press
P.O. Box 3440
Berkeley, CA 94703
www.ulyssespress.com

ISBN: 978-1-61243-842-9
Library of Congress Catalog Number: 2018944070

Printed in the United States by Kingery Printing Company
10 9 8 7 6 5 4

Acquisitions editor: Casie Vogel
Managing editor: Claire Chun
Editor: Shayna Keyles
Proofreader: Renee Rutledge
Cover and interior design: what!design @ whatweb.com
Artwork: cover © TairA/shutterstock.com; interior illustrations © Alisha Boneck; chakra graphics © nuvrenia/
    shutterstock.com
Production: Jake Flaherty

For love

going through the ground and anchoring into the center of the earth. I like to envision it being moved through the dirt and through crystal caves before it finally anchors into the core, but whatever you visualize is just right for you. Once this cord is in place, any energy you absorb throughout the day can be "flushed" down the cord. This can be done quickly and easily by simply closing your eyes, taking a deep breath, and imagining any dirty or negative energy going down the cord to be transmuted into the earth. You can also cut and release this cord at any time, letting it fall away and then creating a new one.

Additionally, you can carry a protective or grounding stone. Wearing a stone such as onyx, tiger's eye, amethyst, hematite, or mugglestone can be beneficial because the vibration these stones emit can help you to feel more stable, calm, and balanced.

I need to have alone time to recharge.

If this sounds like you, provide an example:

_____

_____

_____

_____

_____

It is essential for an empath to spend time alone. An empath cannot and will not thrive in an environment where there is continual stress. This will cause depression, fatigue, self-doubt, physical health issues, anxiety, and a sensation of not being grounded. Empaths can also suffer from sensory overload. This is something that happens when there are too many sensory stimuli, overloading one or more senses. Sensory overload can be triggered when the body tries to process too much information at once, or by loud noises, large crowds, being exposed to stressful situations, and more.

The solution here is to simply allow yourself time to be alone, no matter what. If you are in a relationship, your partner will need to understand that alone time is absolutely necessary for you. This is how an empath quiets their mind, replenishes their energy, and comes back more energized and happier.

For love

Contents

Preface

I had someone tell me a few years ago that through my awakening, I was going to help others in more ways than I could ever imagine. I can certainly tell you, I never thought learning to finally embrace my sensitivities would lead me to publish a book that could help empaths discover who they are and learn to love and embrace their uniqueness. It is my goal that this workbook will help you discover the things that took me a long while to learn and accept. Be true to your emotions and sensitivities. To feel so deeply is a gift, and there truly is a purpose for all of it.

Lots of love and light,

Stephanie

> **"**The ugly duckling is a misunderstood universal myth. It's not about turning into a blonde Barbie doll or becoming what you dream of being; it's about self-revelation, becoming who you are.**"** —Baz Luhrmann

Introduction

Growing up, like many empaths, I always felt different, like I never truly belonged. It never mattered how many times I tried to fit or blend in; I just couldn't. I used to spend a lot of time by myself, often going on long walks or bike rides around water so I could process my emotions and think about life. I would think about what I was doing here, what it all meant, and what I could do to fulfill my purpose as someone who was meant to help others. Though I was certainly not an average kid, I was perfectly content being alone and running around with my shoes off, connecting with nature and everything else around me.

I knew from a very early age that I was not alone and that I could feel subtle energy (I just did not know what it was at the time). I could sense spirit and energy around me often. I remember one day when I was seven or eight years old, I was playing with a Barbie, and recalled a scene from the movie *The NeverEnding Story* when the main character Bastian realized the story he was reading involved him. I remember putting my Barbie down, looking up, and wondering if someone was watching or "reading" about me. No one was there physically, yet I smiled because I felt that there was some sort of divine energy observing me. I knew at that very moment that I was just playing a part in a larger story. Looking back, I realize that this was my first time experiencing the beautiful lesson that separation is an illusion: we are not separate from each other or the divine.

As I grew into my young adult years, like Bastian, I was exposed to situations where I was taught to think first and feel later—which is the total opposite of what an empath naturally does. I was living in a household where this was just simply the way. Unfortunately, because I was taught that I could not trust or depend on my feelings, I started to develop anxiety and suppress my natural connection to my intuition and psychic gifts.

I have noticed that, after working with empaths around the world, many empaths have also experienced anxiety caused from the suppression of their intuition and natural psychic gifts. That is why I've written this book: to help you identify with, support, and develop your beautiful empathic soul and live in alignment with who you truly are.

> "*If you feel as though you don't fit into this world, it is because you are here to help create a new one.*" —Anonymous

How to Use This Book

This workbook has been designed to assist you through the sensitivities and difficulties that can arise in everyday life for an empath. It will also help guide you through some of the common challenges that can be experienced when being moved through the awakening process and learning to embrace empathic gifts, such as heightened intuition.

The information provided in this workbook is all based on information that has come through my experience and knowledge as a fulltime psychic medium, intuitive empath, and certified reiki master. I work with empaths and sensitive souls all around the world.

Use this workbook as a reference guide to help you learn, grow spiritually, and document what you have been or may be experiencing now. Inside, you'll find helpful quizzes, journal prompts, and reflection exercises to help you on your journey of self-discovery. This workbook will also help you connect more to your heart space.

to this phenomenon. Scientists have discovered something called the mirror neuron system.

The mirror neuron system is a group of cells that enable the ability to share another person's emotions such as pain, fear, happiness, or excitement. Mirror neurons are triggered when an individual performs an action, and when that individual sees another person performing the same action. Scientists believe empaths seem to have very sensitive mirror neurons, causing the empath to deeply resonate with other people's emotions.

Electromagnetic fields. It has also been scientifically proven that the heart and the brain generate their own powerful electromagnetic fields that emit information about the thoughts and emotions of others. The heart has been discovered to generate the largest electromagnetic field in the body.

According to the HeartMath Institute, the heart's powerful field can be detected by another up to several feet away. Geomagnetic fields generated by others will certainly affect an empath. The empath may feel a shift, either positive or negative, in their own emotions and physical body, without even realizing that these shifts are not necessarily coming from themselves.

Emotional contagion. Emotional contagion is the phenomenon of instantly picking up on other emotions and experiencing the same emotion. Emotional contagion basically embodies the idea that humans can synchronize their emotions with others around them.

For example, when someone nearby is stressed, fearful, pessimistic, or even angry, an empath can shift quickly out of a very calm state and begin to embody these emotions as well. The same would happen if positive emotions were being expressed.

Interestingly, empaths love to be around other empaths. The energy being exchanged between them is usually very uplifting and of an equal exchange. As an empath, it's important to try to surround yourself with others like you or of a positive nature.

Dopamine sensitivity. Dopamine is a neurotransmitter that helps carry signals to the brain's reward center. It affects emotions and the sensations of pleasure and pain. As Judith Orloff wrote about in her book, *The Empath's Survival Guide*, some empaths have a sensitivity toward dopamine, which means that they need less dopamine to feel happy. These types of empaths are content with less socializing and more alone time. Other, more extroverted empaths may be the exact opposite; they may need to get out so they can socialize to receive a dopamine rush.

Synesthesia. Orloff also describes how empaths are prone to experiencing synesthesia. Synesthesia is a phenomenon that happens when one of the five senses triggers another of the senses to simultaneously process the same data. For example, one may see a color and in addition to seeing the color, the color has a specific smell associated with it. Or, one may hear music and see sounds or colors as they listen to the music.

Mirror touch synesthesia is a blending of the senses. Basically, the things that one sees can be felt. For example, if an empath sees another person's injuries or sufferings, they will also physically feel this pain. If the empath sees another person being touched or experiencing something good, the empath can also feel this.

An empath can experience these types of sensations even if what they are witnessing is just on television or in a movie. If someone hits the ground in a scene, the empath might feel it as if it were happening to them. Mirror touch synesthesia is a beautiful neurological explanation of what empaths experience daily.

CHAPTER TWO

Are You an Empath?

The list of questions below will help you quickly determine if you are energetically sensitive and consider yourself to be an empath. Afterward, you'll find a detailed explanation of how to deal with each of the scenarios the quiz asks about.

Only you will know if you are truly an empath, but if you have this book in your hands, odds are, you are an empath or are checking out the content for someone who is. Take this quiz to see if you might be an empath.

QUIZ: ARE YOU AN EMPATH?

1. Do you have a hard time being around a lot of people? Does a feeling of exhaustion come over you after being in a large crowd?

    ○ YES   ○ NO

2. You need to have your alone time. It is essential for you to recharge. Often, after exerting yourself, you feel as though you need a whole day to simply get back into balance with yourself.

    ○ YES   ○ NO

3. Do you have a hard time with harsh lighting, such as florescent lighting in an office or grocery store? What about loud noises?

    ○ YES   ○ NO

4. Do you absorb and take on other people's emotions and stress?

    ○ YES   ○ NO

5. Does being outside, walking barefoot, and connecting with nature feel like an essential part of your life?

    ○ YES   ○ NO

6. Are you a nurturer or "motherer" to your family and friends? Always making sure everyone is taken care of, even at the expense of your own wellbeing? A true people pleaser and healer?

    ○ YES   ○ NO

7. Have you ever been labeled as too sensitive or too emotional?

    ○ YES   ○ NO

8. Do you experience unexpected anxiety? It may feel like unexplained energy, centered in your chest, that hits you out of nowhere. I often describe this feeling as hundreds of butterflies flying around inside of me.

    ○ YES   ○ NO

9. Do you have a hard time with confrontation and arguments to the extent that you might feel physically ill in such situations? ◯ YES ◯ NO

10. Do you have a hard time seeing negative or harsh images on television and movies; for example, people hurting other people or animals? ◯ YES ◯ NO

11. Do you have intuitive gifts such as clairvoyance, clairsentience, claircognizance, and clairaudience (see page 30)? ◯ YES ◯ NO

12. Do you find yourself attracting people who are in need of emotional support? Are you the person who everyone seems to come to for advice, support, and healing? You may even find that strangers will just start telling you their life story. ◯ YES ◯ NO

13. Do you sense when people need things, or understand the thoughts of others? Have you ever had people tell you to "get out of their heads"? ◯ YES ◯ NO

14. Do you feel other people's emotions and pain, taking on their energetic mood swings as your own, especially if they are nearby? ◯ YES ◯ NO

15. Do you have a hard time with self-love and boundaries, attracting narcissistic people and allowing them to drain you of your energy? ◯ YES ◯ NO

16. Are you attracted to alternative healing such as reiki, intuitive healing, meditation, or anything else holistic? ◯ YES ◯ NO

17. Do you hold your feelings to yourself for fear that it will upset others in your life, even if you know that what you are feeling so strongly is true? Do you worry about rocking the boat and creating negative energy?

◯ YES   ◯ NO

If you answered yes to 10 or more of these questions, you're probably an empath. On the following pages, we'll look at each question individually and discuss techniques for addressing them in daily life.

I have a hard time being around a lot of people.

If this sounds like you, provide an example:

_____

_____

_____

_____

_____

Because empaths have the beautiful ability to absorb and transmute the emotions and energy of other people, it is very important to make sure you, as an empath, are grounded and shielded if you know you are going to be around a lot of people. Here are some suggestions to help protect your energy.

If you know you are going to be around a crowd, start by doing a nice grounding meditation. I recommend working on your root chakra (see page 123), but any of the lower chakras are fine. You can use a power crystal, such as obsidian or petrified wood, to help you anchor this grounding energy. If it is warm enough, go outside and complete your meditation out on the grass.

You can also cord and anchor into the earth. This is an essential exercise for any empath to practice daily, and is easy to do every morning when you wake up. Envision a beautiful white or gold light coming down from heaven in through the top of your head (your crown chakra), and allow it to wash down through your body and out through the bottom of your feet. Once the light/cord has moved out of the bottom of your feet, imagine it going through the ground and anchoring into the center of the earth. I like to envision it being moved through the dirt and through crystal caves before it finally anchors into the core, but whatever you visualize is just right for you. Once this cord is in place, any energy you absorb throughout the day can be "flushed" down the cord. This can be done quickly and easily by simply closing your eyes, taking a deep breath, and imagining any dirty or negative energy going down the cord to be transmuted into the earth. You can also cut and release this cord at any time, letting it fall away and then creating a new one.

Additionally, you can carry a protective or grounding stone. Wearing a stone such as onyx, tiger's eye, amethyst, hematite, or mugglestone can be beneficial because the vibration these stones emit can help you to feel more stable, calm, and balanced.

I need to have alone time to recharge.

If this sounds like you, provide an example:

_____

_____

_____

_____

_____

It is essential for an empath to spend time alone. An empath cannot and will not thrive in an environment where there is continual stress. This will cause depression, fatigue, self-doubt, physical health issues, anxiety, and a sensation of not being grounded. Empaths can also suffer from sensory overload. This is something that happens when there are too many sensory stimuli, overloading one or more senses. Sensory overload can be triggered when the body tries to process too much information at once, or by loud noises, large crowds, being exposed to stressful situations, and more.

The solution here is to simply allow yourself time to be alone, no matter what. If you are in a relationship, your partner will need to understand that alone time is absolutely necessary for you. This is how an empath quiets their mind, replenishes their energy, and comes back more energized and happier.

During your alone time, it is important to do anything you can that simply helps you to feel good. Every empath is different, and alone-time practices will vary. However, I recommend meditating, being creative, visiting nature, sleeping, taking an Epsom salt bath, or simply allowing yourself to just exist. These activities are vital to an empath's mental and physical health. Do not deny yourself, or allow others to deny you, your alone time.

I have difficulty with harsh lighting and noises.

If this sounds like you, provide an example:

_____

_____

_____

_____

_____

Empaths usually enjoy calm and natural or low levels of light, so harsh lighting is something that they battle with often. Sitting in an office environment with nothing but harsh lighting all day will cause tension and exhaustion for the empath. The best advice I can give you here is to avoid it as much as you possibly can. Some empaths will use light-reducing glasses while in the workplace. At home, many empaths enjoy and prefer soft lighting. Using lamps or utilizing dimmer switches can help an empath feel calmer and more at peace. Many empaths also enjoy candles.

Empaths also prefer quiet, soft, and controllable noise levels. This is not to say that an empath won't enjoy a concert now and again; however, they will feel the energy drain from them once it is over and for a few days afterward. Loud noises such as a revved-up motorcycle going by on the street is basically like soul shock to the empath and will cause tension immediately. Empaths need quiet. It is essential to their wellbeing.

I feel like I absorb other people's emotions and stress.

If this sounds like you, provide an example:

_____

_____

_____

_____

_____

Empaths are so energetically sensitive that they can feel the emotions and ailments of everyone around them, especially if they are not aware of what they are and how to protect themselves. An empath can even take on someone's negative energy and transmute it into something positive. This is great for the other person, but exhausting for the empath. So if you are surrounded by lots of people and you are not protecting your own energy, you are opening yourself up and inviting other people into your space.

It is so important for an empath to set boundaries and not allow themselves to take on other people's stress and emotions. If you find yourself taking on the emotions of others and that these emotional experiences are not serving you, set a boundary and release yourself from the situation, whether for the moment or forever. Learn more about boundary setting on page 50.

If you begin to feel overwhelmed by energies, stop for a moment, take a few deep breaths, and ask yourself "Is this mine?". If it doesn't actually feel like your stuff, imagine breathing in white light and blowing the energy right out of you or back toward the person it is coming from.

Set healthy boundaries. This is huge! Only engage with people who make you feel good and empower you. Right away, you will know who does and who doesn't. If you find yourself in a situation where you cannot avoid a negative encounter, stop, take a deep breath, and again, blow away the energy because it is not yours, it is the projection of the other person who was trying to impress upon you.

If you notice that you feel better around some people and not so good around others, you may be involved with an energy vampire. This topic is explored on page 72.

I love being outside and connecting with nature.

If this sounds like you, provide an example:

_____

_____

_____

_____

Empaths love connecting with nature, especially water; it is like a drug for them. Empaths usually love when it rains, as this provides them with an extreme sense of calm. Get outside as much as possible, especially if you are having a hard time feeling grounded. Hiking, walking, bike riding, camping, exploring, or just simply being out in the sun is essential for empaths to reconnect and ground.

I nurture my friends and family, making sure that everyone is taken care of. Sometimes I do this at the expense of my own wellbeing.

If this sounds like you, provide an example:

_____

_____

_____

_____

As stated before, empaths are natural healers and want to help others. Your friends and family are going to be drawn to your natural healing and empathic gifts. As long as you are setting healthy boundaries and protecting yourself from taking on the issues presented by your loved ones, you will be fine. Just remember, if you feel overwhelmed at all, it's time to do an energy check and ask yourself what you need to do to avoid processing someone else's emotions for them, so you can help them process these things themselves.

It is crucial for an empath to learn to care for themselves first before helping others—in other words, make sure your cup is full before serving others. You are worth the effort. If an empath does not learn this vital lesson, they will often feel burnt out or even develop codependent types of behavior with others in their life (page 74).

If filling up your own cup first upsets others in your life, then it may be time for you to reassess who is being allowed into your energy field.

I have been called "too sensitive" or "too emotional."
If this sounds like you, provide an example:

_____

_____

_____

_____

_____

Empaths are often labeled as "too sensitive" or "too emotional." But, this is often because the empath may not know how to protect their energy when they are around others or the empath is simply not grounded. Or, other people who don't understand what the empath is feeling and how empaths process emotions may call an empath "too sensitive."

Not only does the empath have to process their own emotions, the empath will pick up and carry the emotions of others. When the empath can no longer carry every emotion and they feel the need to release, they will just let out everything they have been feeling (or suppressing) all at once. This can confuse others, who don't understand what the empath has been processing and trying to transmute.

So what can you do in this situation? Protect your energy and stay grounded. If you are around people or involved in a situation that is not serving you, set an immediate boundary or leave the situation.

Remember to allow yourself to feel all that you are feeling and processing. Your emotions and that subtle energy that you are sensing is trying to tell you something. Listen and then act accordingly. Know that your "sensitivities" are a gift and they are to be treated that way. There is nothing wrong with you, sometimes you are simply picking up on and processing subtle energy that others may not understand.

Sometimes I have unexpected anxiety or a heightened level of energy that I cannot explain.

If this sounds like you, provide an example:

_____

_____

_____

_____

_____

I have seen this symptom occur with a lot of empaths. It seems to come on when the empath has not been listening to their intuition or picking up on energy from a loved one that is thinking about them.

If you are feeling this way, here are a few things that can help ease that feeling.

First, always honor what you are feeling. As an empath, you are much more intuitive and psychic than you give yourself credit for. Remember that your intuition is trying to tell you something. Listen to your inner voice by meditating, taking a moment to ground yourself, or praying. When you are anxious, take a few deep breaths and come back into the moment. It is important to be present so you can distinguish what is going on, but you must first be grounded to do this. A lot of empaths question their psychic gifts; however, these empaths are usually the most gifted and should trust themselves the most.

If the anxious energy you feel seems to be associated with a connection you have with another person, take a deep breath, imagine breathing in some white/gold light, and simply blow the energy you are receiving back toward its origin.

It is difficult for me to handle confrontation and arguments.

If this sounds like you, provide an example:

_____

_____

_____

_____

Empaths have a very hard time handling this type of energy exchange without feeling physically ill. You will find that most empaths will not be able to have a "fair" argument because the empath will feel so drained that words will not be able to come out of their mouths. If they are able to speak, their words will likely be jumbled; the empath may be too taken aback by the intense exchange of energy to fight back.

At some point on their journey, an empath will be moved through an argument or confrontation. Here are a few tips that may help the process run a little smoother.

Stay grounded so you can think clearly (learn about grounding on page 138). Do not allow the other party to completely take over your energy field; protect your space. Do not allow the other party to project their own issues onto you. Explain to the other party how much the negative energy exchange is affecting you and ask if there is another way the matter can be handled. If the other party does not stop or does not respect your mutual connection enough to honor what you are saying, then you may need to reassess how much time you spend around this individual. This may be a lesson in boundaries for the empath (see page 50).

If you cannot handle the situation, there is no shame in that. It may be best to leave. You are under no obligation to sit there and fight with another. Ask yourself, "Is this worth my energy?" It is very common for an empath to simply walk away instead of arguing with another individual who will not stop until they win. Empaths are not fighters; they are lovers. When an empath is exposed to an argument or negative/fear-based energy exchange, the empath will literally feel as though they are suffocating and need to get out of the situation fast.

It is difficult for me to see negative or harsh images on television and in movies.

If this sounds like you, provide an example:

_____

_____

_____

_____

This is very common for empaths. My advice here is to simply limit the amount of time spent watching this type of imagery, or to remove watching negative shows altogether. If it does not make you feel good, don't watch it. Sometimes an image that an empath is exposed to can trigger the empath in days to follow, so it is best to limit the negativity intake that you have control over.

I have intuitive gifts or I find myself drawn to others with intuitive gifts.

If this sounds like you, provide an example:

_____

_____

_____

_____

Like attracts like—it is a simple law. If you find yourself being drawn to psychics and other healers, odds are that you, too, are a healer or have some sort of psychic gift that you may be suppressing.

I find myself attracting people in need of emotional support.

If this sounds like you, provide an example:

_____

_____

_____

_____

This is totally normal. Healers attract people who need healing. Get used to it: It will happen more and more, especially as your gifts expand. The key here is to make sure your cup is always full before helping others heal.

It is important to know that not everyone can be healed. This is a big lesson that many empaths and healers will be moved through at some point on their journey. If you are attracting toxic people, it is best to simply place up a boundary and stop extending your energy toward them. This may not feel good at first, but is essential for your overall well-being. Not all people or situations can be healed.

I can tell when other people need things; sometimes, people tell me to "get out of their heads."

If this sounds like you, provide an example:

_____

_____

_____

_____

This is a common experience for empaths. For example, you can be in another room of the house and know if a family member or friend needs something without them even saying anything. At times, you may have had these people tell you to "get out of their head."

Honor what you are feeling. Play with it. If you are feeling the need to call someone, bring someone aspirin, or whatever else it may be, do it. You are feeling it for a reason. It may not feel like anything special to you, but I promise, after doing this a few times, you will most likely shock yourself and the other person involved.

I can feel the pain and emotions of others.

If this sounds like you, provide an example:

_____

_____

_____

_____

_____

This is also a common experience for empaths. For example, when you are by yourself, you feel fine and in touch with who you are, but when you are around someone who is not feeling well on the inside, you feel it as if their pain is your own. Then, you may take on their pain and try to fix it as if it were your own. When you are not around this person for a few days, you feel totally fine.

It is a beautiful gift to be able to feel so deeply and be so in tune with the other people, especially if you are on the path of becoming, or already are, an intuitive healer of some kind. However, the key here is to check your energy before and after you are around other people. Trust that if you are not feeling good energetically, then a person or situation with a strong emotional pull will literally drain your energy. In these cases, healthy boundaries need to be set or cords may need to be severed.

It is difficult for me to set boundaries. I feel like I attract unhealthy or codependent people or situations.

If this sounds like you, provide an example:

_____

_____

_____

_____

_____

Empaths tend to do a little dance with narcissists and unhealthy or manipulative people. Often, because empaths are natural healers, they will feel like they can fix every situation or person that comes across their path, causing them to form relationships with these unhealthy individuals. Unfortunately, empaths are known to beat themselves up if they cannot fix a situation, so they will often stay in a toxic situation far beyond the expiration date.

Unhealthy situations will keep repeating themselves until an empath learns their own value. The key to getting out of these situations is to surrender. Surrender to what you cannot change and get yourself out of or away from the negative situation or person. Do not fall for manipulation, and trust yourself. A narcissistic person, or energetic vampire, will do everything they can to instill doubt in the empath. They will play on the empath's emotions and make them feel like they are doing something wrong, or try to make the empath feel guilty for putting themselves first. Don't allow this. You are a diamond, and the negative people using you to boost themselves up are aware of this; you just need to learn this for yourself.

I am attracted to alternative healing practices.

If this sounds like you, provide an example:

_____

_____

_____

_____

It is natural for an empath to be attracted to anything related to energy. Allow yourself to be drawn to what you are intuitively drawn to when it comes to alternative and energy healing. This will gently open you up to learning that there is more than just this physical world. In fact, reiki changed my life and played a key role in my initial healing and awakening. I encourage everyone to receive or learn reiki/alternative healing methods.

I keep things to myself, even when I am feeling them incredibly deeply, so I won't upset others.

If this sounds like you, provide an example:

_____

_____

_____

_____

Your sensitivity is a gift and your feelings need to be expressed and honored. This is a vital part of self-love and setting healthy boundaries for yourself. If you are scared to express yourself, you are most likely around the wrong people and involved in a possible codependent situation. This is the perfect opportunity for you to empower yourself, and there is nothing more beautiful than an empowered empath. This is an essential lesson an empath must learn.

I first started expressing myself by simply honoring how I felt and speaking up more about what I was feeling at the time. I stopped allowing anyone to dismiss my feelings or intuitive nudges. This is a great place to start. Day by day, I grew stronger, and expressing myself wasn't as hard. This also led me to learn how to set healthy boundaries for myself.

CHAPTER THREE

What Is Your Empath Gift?

There is more than one type of empath gift, which is an ability that an empath possesses. It is totally possible to embody one or all of these gifts. I identify with many of these gifts, myself. You may identify with one empath gift more strongly than you identify with another; this is totally fine.

Having a strong emotional sense is an example of an empath gift. If you have this empath gift, you are called an "emotional empath." Emotional empaths tend to be the most common type. Other types of empaths include physical empaths, intuitive/psychic empaths, earth empaths, and animal empaths.

Emotional Empath

You are a sponge for other people's energy and emotions. You will feel terrible when you are around some people and highly energized when around others. Let's say your spouse, family member, or friend suffers from anxiety or depression. You will feel totally fine when you are alone, but when you are around this person, you begin to take on these symptoms and feel like you are the one with anxiety or depression. Another example is being around someone with an extremely positive energy. After spending time with this person, you will walk away feeling wonderful, like the energy exchange shared between the two of you was equal.

Is this you? Provide an example of your experience:

_____

_____

_____

_____

Physical Empath

You take on and feel the physical ailments of other people. Let's say your spouse, family member, or friend suffers from physical pain. Before you know it, you also begin to feel the same pain or discomfort. Sometimes, you take it on and they feel better. Some physical empaths can also run their hands over the other person and feel the energy or lack thereof coming out of the other person. A lot of reiki healers are physical empaths.

Is this you? Provide an example of your experience:

_____

_____

_____

_____

Intuitive Empath

Intuitive empaths are not only energetically sensitive; they are often psychic, receiving messages through their dreams early on. They tend to have beautiful precognitive gifts and are often very telepathic. An example of these gifts are below.

Intuitive dreaming. Intuitive empaths are usually clairvoyant, and their dreams often contain guidance with answers to questions or solutions to any issues they may be experiencing. More often than not, the empath will even receive messages from their spiritual team (such as spirit guides or angels) and from those who have passed. The conversations will be as clear as if you were speaking with them in the physical.

Intuitive dreamers may also experience precognitive experiences while in dream state. For example, I had a few experiences when I was a young adult where relatives who had passed would come through into my dream space and tell me where to find pieces of jewelry or family photographs that had been missing for a while. I also had a very specific dream where I saw my mother's Chihuahua and a snake. I mentioned this to her and sure enough, a few days later, she found a long black snake in her backyard.

Astral projection. Intuitive dreamers may experience astral projection, which is when you leave your physical body and hover over your environment. The only way I can describe my experiences with this is falling asleep, and then looking down at myself in bed. I would be wearing the same clothes, sleeping in the same position, yet I was floating over myself. If this happens to you, there is no need to be scared or worried. It seems to be a normal thing that many intuitive empaths experience.

Precognition. Intuitive empaths also have the gift of knowing when things are going to happen in the future. This can happen while you are awake or while you are dreaming. If this happens to you, take these impressions seriously, this is a gift. There have been several times on my journey where these premonitions have come true within hours or days of me having a dream or vision.

Is this you? Provide an example of your experience:

_____

_____

_____

_____

Telepathic Empath

A telepathic empath will receive what I like to call thought impressions being exchanged with another person. These impressions can feel like flashes from a movie while the empath is awake. The impression is an indicator about thoughts being exchanged between the two as well as something that may be going on in "real time." For example: The empath will have a strong impression of a friend being at the door and then moments later, that very person rings the doorbell. Another example would be receiving an impression of a friend or family member being ill, then later finding out that they actually are ill.

Is this you? Provide an example of your experience:

_____

_____

_____

_____

Mediums

An empath with this ability has the gift to be able to communicate with those who have crossed over and are vibrating at a higher level. The empath will be able to hear, feel, and sense what spirit is communicating with them. The name medium actually comes from the empath raising their vibration enough to connect with spirit and spirit lowering their vibration enough to make the connection between the two—thus, a medium-level vibration is created.

Is this you? Provide an example of your experience:

_____

_____

_____

_____

_____

Nature/Earth Empath

Nature empaths tend to be very connected with Mother Nature. They are very sensitive to weather patterns and planetary movements. I have heard of some nature empaths who are so in tune that they will feel much sadness right before a major catastrophe hits somewhere on the planet. Although this is not something I have a lot of experience with personally, I have witnessed other empaths go through similar events like this. Some empaths even have a hard time when thunderstorms come in, when they hear loud noises associated with any kind of storm or feel wind of any kind.

Animal empaths are a type of nature/earth empath. Animal empaths can pick up on the energies emitted by an animal. A famous animal empath is Sonja Fitzpatrick. Sonja has the ability to be able to communicate with and pick up what animals are feeling.

Is this you? Provide an example of an experience like this:

_____

_____

_____

_____

All about Clairs

A clair refers to an individual's heightened intuitive or physical senses. A clair is a gift that allows an individual to have psychic knowledge that defies logic or has no explanation. In addition to their empath gifts, some empaths may develop clairs.

Clairvoyance

Clairvoyance is clear seeing. You see things not just in the dream world, but while you are awake. People with this gift often confuse the guidance they are receiving through clairvoyance with daydreaming. They may believe that they are just thinking too much and random images are showing up while they are going about their day. However, often, this "daydreaming" is actually impressions of possible outcomes and timelines.

A lot of people who do not realize that they are clairvoyant think that the things they see are things that everyone else sees. However, this is not the case. Clairvoyants are born this way, so they do not realize until later that they are seeing things very differently than others do—not only in the physical world, but in their mind's eye, as well.

Clairvoyants are incredibly visual. They see everything in pictures, symbols, colors, or signs. The gift of clairvoyance also comes with the ability to see energy around others. Someone with the gift of clairvoyance may find themselves seeing colors or sparks of light around other people. A clairvoyant may also see those who have passed, or find themselves catching images out of the corner of their eyes. Many clairvoyants see energy moving very quickly, like an orb or a flash of color across the room.

For example, from the time I was a young girl, I would see colors or what I could only describe as outlines of energy in my home. As I got older, I saw my grandfather who had passed sitting at the edge of my bed one evening, a man and a small child standing on the staircase of a home I purchased, and my spouse's grandmother standing in my bedroom doorway. All of these events happened very quickly, when I least expected it. It's important to note that this is how these experiences typically begin—quickly, like a flash.

To further develop your clairvoyant gifts, I encourage you to spend time in daily meditation with a journal. Write down everything that you see—and I mean everything, even the things that you do not understand right away. There is a reason you are seeing these things. You may be seeing your loved ones or their spirits, for example. At first, your ego will try to talk you out of what you are seeing, and that is okay. Just allow these things to happen, and don't become attached to what you think you are supposed to be experiencing. What you are meant to see will be seen. For those of you who would like to take a more spiritual approach, you can call upon your spiritual team or Archangel Raziel to help you develop this clair. (See Chapter 8.)

MEDITATION EXERCISE

Sit down in meditation pose with your back straight (see Chapter 9 for more on meditation, including a beginner's exercise). Aim to be nice and relaxed. Inhale with deep, slow, calm breaths. Put on some beautiful meditation music and allow yourself to simply be. Close your eyes and go for as long as you feel guided. You can hold a pen in one of your hands and write down what you see while meditating. Keeping a journal next to you is going to be important.

Write down what you experience during meditation either below or in your journal. You will feel refreshed and your rational mind will love seeing how the messages come together and mesh with what you are experiencing in your life right at the moment. Simply using the internet to look up the spiritual meaning of the images you see will give you plenty of information to start with and expand on.

_____

_____

_____

_____

_____

Clairaudience

Clairaudience is clear hearing. You hear things that the average person cannot hear. It can start with messages in music (a lot of musicians are clairaudient) or movies, or you may simply hear the same message over and over again from different sources. You will notice very quickly how synchronistic the messages are and how often, they are the answers to what you need to know.

As you develop, you will begin to notice that your gift of clairaudience will turn into more than just external hearing. You will need to learn the difference between your own thoughts and a thought that is impressed upon you. An "inner hearing" will begin to develop aside from the external hearing.

To further develop your clairaudient gifts I encourage you to take time out to simply listen every day. Listen to everything going on around you. All of it. Meditation, listening to binaural beats, reiki treatments, and clearing of the ear chakras will also be beneficial. Those of you who would like to take a more spiritual approach can call upon your team or Archangel Zadkiel, to help you develop this clair. (See Chapter 8.)

LISTENING EXERCISE

Something that really helped me in the beginning was going out and sitting in my backyard, closing my eyes, and practicing what I like to call a silent meditation. I listened to everything going on around me without vision. I could hear things that I never really noticed before. You will notice every bird chirp, traffic going by, wind, people in action—everything and anything. The important thing to take note of is how many things you can listen to all at once while still hearing it all. Take note of what sounds may be standing out to you more than the others. Are you noticing that you are hearing a bird more than the traffic going by? Allow yourself to observe all of it and truly listen. Write down what you experienced below and keep repeating this exercise as you feel guided.

_____

_____

_____

_____

Clairsentience

Clairsentience is clear feeling. You feel so deeply that sometimes it feels like feeling is all you know how to do. You can also feel emotions of others. You will most likely be able to feel if there are other energies in the room with you as well. This is a very common clair for empaths to have strength in.

It is important to pay attention to how you are feeling because this is often divine guidance you are receiving.

To further develop your clairsentient gifts I encourage you to trust in what you are feeling. Always. For those of you who would like to take a more spiritual approach, call upon your team or Archangel Raguel, to help you develop this clair. (See Chapter 8.)

FEELING EXERCISE

Use the art of discernment to check in with how you are feeling about a situation in your life. Close your eyes, place your hands on your heart, and ask if everything feels right or if there is another way you should be going. It really is that easy, asking your heart. It's usually the mind that complicates, and clairsentience is all about the heart—feeling, not thinking. If an emotion resonates with you, it is meant for you. You will notice that when you are in your heart space, clarity comes very quickly, every time. Write down what you experienced below and keep repeating this exercise as you feel guided.

_____

_____

_____

_____

Claircognizance

Claircognizance is clear knowing. Many analytical people and problem solvers, like doctors, scientists, and lawyers, are extremely claircognizant. If you are claircognizant, you simply know the answer to things, or you receive your answers and guidance through repetitive thoughts and ideas. No, it is not wishful thinking or random thoughts popping into your head. If you keep thinking about something, there is a reason for it. The information you receive comes through precisely and clearly. You just know something—you don't know how, but you trust it and go with it.

To further develop your claircognizant gifts, I encourage you to pay attention to the recurring new and inspiring ideas you are having on a regular basis. For example, if you keep having an idea to start a new business or project and are constantly coming up with strategies to make it work, it's highly likely that you are receiving guidance to move toward what is meant for you next on your journey. For those of you who would like to take a more spiritual approach, you can call upon your team or Archangel Uriel to help you develop this clair. (See Chapter 8.)

THINKING EXERCISE

Journaling your thoughts and ideas are an excellent way to develop your claircognizant gifts. You can even write down a question and then see what the very first answer is that comes up in your mind. The key is trusting in the very first answer you receive, without doubt. Practice this exercise daily. Take a moment to ask yourself a question now, such as "What do I really want?" or "What step should I take next?" Then, write down what you experienced below. Keep repeating this exercise as you feel guided.

_____

_____

_____

_____

Developing Your Empath Gift

The more you honor and pay attention to the guidance that comes through your dreams or any other ability you have, the more you will begin to trust what you experience. Talk about your gifts and sensitivities openly with those closest to you. This really helps you wrap your logical mind around what you are experiencing. Keep a journal (this really helps you wrap your logical mind around what you are experiencing) and ask your spiritual and physical team (including friends and family) to help you remember and trust in the guidance that comes through. Go with the flow and have fun with your development.

CHAPTER FOUR

Energy and Emotion

We live in a world that is made up of different types of energy. Nothing is truly solid. Everything you see in the physical world, including you, is simply vibrating at different frequencies.

You, the ones you love, and the rest of us living on this planet are energetic beings. We each have our own frequency that we carry at different times of the day, the night, and at different points or experiences along our individual journeys. The emotions of love and fear also have their own frequency.

The feelings and thoughts that we have also carry energy. When we feel good or think positively, we emit positive energy. When we feel bad or think negatively, we emit negative energy. Whatever energetic pattern or frequency we carry internally manifests itself externally into physical reality. We are truly that powerful. This is not a conceptual way of thinking; this is quantum physics. Quantum physics has revealed what the ancient masters once knew: The substance of the universe is consciousness.

Manifesting and Emotions

Human beings are made of billions of atoms, known as the building blocks of the universe. An atom is one of the smallest units of matter, made up of protons, neutrons, and electrons. When atoms are balanced, it is due to energy. Albert Einstein and Max Planck spent a good portion of their careers working on this.

What all this means is that human beings naturally create energy. Scientists now believe that energy stems from consciousness and that there is a direct connection between consciousness and the physical/material world. Experiments have been conducted to learn more about this connection.

At Princeton University, for example, three hundred participants were asked to observe a computer screen that had two images alternating on it: an astronaut and a leopard. When the participants were asked which image they preferred, the majority ruled in favor of the astronaut.

Once the preferred image was discovered, the participants were asked to solely focus on the astronaut. They were asked to make it their intention that only the astronaut appear. The two images rotated around for a little while longer, but once the participants focused just a little longer on what they wanted to see, the image of the astronaut was the only image that appeared repeatedly. The experiment ended and it was concluded that with conscious influence, the physical world could be altered.

Make it your intention to focus on what you want, live in a higher vibration, and watch your physical world shift and rearrange itself for you. Just remember that as a human being, you are sending out an energetic pattern always. As an empath, you are constantly absorbing and transmuting energy, so it is important to do what you can to keep your vibration high, so you can consciously create.

> **"***If you want to know the secrets of the universe, think in terms of energy, frequency, and vibration.***"** —Nikola Tesla

One of the most important things to remember is that our emotions help shape our reality. The key to manifesting our desires is to become a vibrational match for those desires.

If you learn how to wisely use the power of your emotions and your gifts of deep feeling, you can master the art of manifesting. What you desire is the key to aligning with your soul's journey. We desire what we do for a reason; we are meant to experience all of it. We just have to believe it.

Exercises for Manifesting

1. Spend a minimum of five minutes daily focusing on your desire. I like to do this during my regular meditation sessions.

Close your eyes, take a nice deep breath in, and focus on your heart space. Begin to focus all of your energy on what that beautiful heart is desiring. Use your imagination to visualize yourself achieving the goals you want to achieve: driving a new car, attaining new clients, or changing careers.

How does it feel?

_____

_____

_____

Hold on to that feeling and keep visualizing it as reality. Believe that it is possible. See yourself celebrating and feeling good as you enjoy your manifestation.

What do you want to manifest?

_____

_____

_____

_____

_____

Do you believe that it's possible? Why?

_____

_____

_____

_____

_____

2. Practice gratitude for at least five minutes a day. When we focus on what we are grateful for, we naturally send out a higher vibration to the universe. We affirm what we are loving, which then sends a message to the universe to deliver us more.

Close your eyes, take a nice deep breath, and focus on your heart space. Ask yourself, "What am I grateful for?" Repeat this over and over again. I like to do this during my regular meditation sessions.

What are you grateful for?

_____

_____

_____

_____

_____

3. Keep that vibration high! Stay in alignment with your desires—no fear-based thinking or living. Love and fear do not live in the same place.

Choose positive thoughts, choose to speak positively, and do not allow anything to keep you from manifesting your desires. If you have a negative thought, say out loud "It's ok that I had that thought," and then think about what you desire or what you are grateful for.

> ❝ *Those who live from their heart can manifest the life of their dreams. Those who live from their head can also manifest, but will ultimately still wonder why they are not fulfilled.* ❞ —Unknown

How Emotions Affect Our Overall Health

The quality of our overall emotions is what determines the instructions that our heart sends to our brain. So when we are living in a low, fear-based vibrational energy (judgment, grief, jealousy, or hate), our heart sends our brain a signal of chaos, which causes us to go into a fight-or-flight response. Someone living in fear may experience depression, anxiety, muscle pain, obesity, digestive disorders, immune system suppression, headaches, and migraines.

However, when we are living in a high vibrational energy, such as love (gratitude, hope, trust, faith), a different type of signal is sent to our brains that is more regular, soft, smooth, and serving. In the presence of positive emotions, such as appreciation, gratitude, compassion, and caring, our brain releases a very different kind of chemistry into the body. When we feel a sense of wellbeing, the level of stress hormones in our bodies decreases, while the life-affirming chemistry of a powerful immune system with anti-aging properties increases.

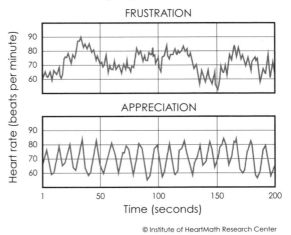

Changing Heart Rhythms

© Institute of HeartMath Research Center

The shift between the stress response and a feeling of wellbeing can happen quickly.

According to Gregg Braden, American author and scholar, "an individual living in alignment with fear (negative emotions) is limited to the number of antenna that is available to them." On the other hand, an individual living in alignment with the feelings of love (positive emotions) has many more opportunities to connect with their intuition. This means it is a lot harder to connect with your intuition and trust in your own feelings and gifts when you are living in a constant state of fear and worry.

To change your vibrational pattern, you will need to base your emotions in love rather than fear. That requires a total shift in consciousness. When you do this, you change your brain chemistry and your personal vibration rises. This provides more opportunities to connect to your wisdom within and allows your intuition to strengthen.

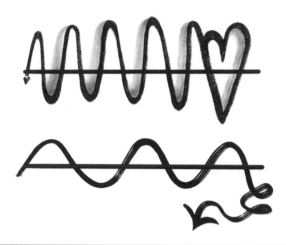

When we live in alignment with love, we have more opportunities to connect with our own vibration and the divine, infinite wisdom held inside of our heart. This ultimately gives us the clarity that we need to create our own reality and align with the blueprint of our soul's journey.

Cymatics, Love, and Fear

Cymatics is the study of vibration. It allows us to see the vibrational patterns that sound creates in the physical world. Because of cymatics, we can see what the high vibrational pattern of love looks like, we can also see what the low vibrational pattern of fear looks like when it manifests. Yes, love and fear vibrate in two totally different places. It is impossible for love and fear to vibrate in the same place, and this has now been scientifically proven. A high vibrational frequency and a low vibrational frequency create two totally different patterns that are then manifested into matter.

The science behind all of this started way back in the late 1700s when Ernst Chladni, a German physicist and musician, published a study called "Discoveries in the Theory of Sound." Chladni described patterns that showed up in sand placed on metal plates when he stroked the edge of these metal plates with his bow. This motion emitted a frequency, which caused the structure of the matter to change.

Hans Jenny was a Swiss scientist inspired by Chladni's work; he coined the term "cymatics." Jenny discovered how the frequency of sound and vibration changed the shape of all kinds of matter, including liquid, plastic, pastes, and more. He documented the effects via photography.

Empaths and Cymatics

Empaths are consistently tuning into the vibration and frequencies of others and of their environment every day, all day long. When an empath makes the conscious decision to raise their own personal vibrational frequency by honoring and loving themselves more, the empath will see positive changes in their physical reality. It is up to an empath to decide whether they are going to continue to feel "like their gifts are a curse," or embrace and love their sensitivities.

An empath must learn the crucial lesson of surrounding themselves with energy that only serves them. When an empath fails to set healthy boundaries, allows themselves to stay unbalanced, gives their energy away, focuses on pleasing others, and consciously decides to live in alignment with the vibration of fear, they will not be able to tune into their own vibration or strengthen their intuition. This often results in creating a negative pattern for themselves.

Remember that you know what serves you and what doesn't. Your gifts have been given to you to help yourself and others live in alignment with the vibration of love. Ask yourself daily: "Am I choosing to live in alignment with love or fear?"

Look at this chart and ask yourself how many times a day you align with these feelings. Our emotions are a map, and they let us know when we are in or out of alignment.

When doing this exercise, it is important to honor all that you felt throughout the week and not beat yourself up if you noticed that you were more in alignment with fear, because your fear-based emotions are an indicator that something needs to change.

Love-Based Feelings		Fear-Based Feelings	
Love	Hope	Worry	Doubt
Happiness	Gratitude	Blame	Envy/Jealousy
Freedom	Courage	Denial	Judgment
Patience	Trust	Anger	Victimhood

For the next week, write down which emotions you are choosing to align with:

Monday: _____

_____

Tuesday: _____

_____

Wednesday: _____

_____

Thursday: _____

_____

Friday: _____

_____

Saturday: _____

_____

Sunday: _____

_____

What did I choose to align with more this week? Love, or fear? _____

If I am choosing to align with fear-based feelings, what is causing this? And how can I shift this for myself so I feel more in alignment and empowered?

_____

_____

_____

_____

_____

_____

If I am choosing to align with love-based feelings, what do I need to keep doing to stay in balance and keep my vibration high?

_____

_____

_____

_____

_____

Binaural Beats and the Effects on the Physical Body

Our brains produce waves of different frequencies, also known as brainwaves. The higher the brainwave frequency is, the more awake and energized we feel. At lower brainwave frequencies, we experience a state of rest or even asleep.

In 1837, a physicist named Heinrich Wilhelm Dove discovered that listening to specific tones can induce a state of mind. Binaural beats are a type of tone that can do this; they are created when the brain is presented with two different frequencies at the same time. Binaural beat research shows that we can change how we feel by listening to different binaural beat frequencies.

Research by Dr. Vincent Giampapa, former president of American Board of Anti-Aging, suggested that binaural beats positively affect three hormones that directly relate to overall wellbeing: cortisol, DHEA, and melatonin. Cortisol is found in the adrenal glands and affects our stress responses. DHEA helps our immune system and other functions, and melatonin helps regulate our sleep. Typically, we want lower cortisol levels, and higher levels of DHEA and melatonin. Dr. Giampapa found that when using binaural beats, cortisol levels went down by an average of 46 percent, DHEA increased by an average of 43 percent, and melatonin production was increased by an average of 98 percent. Other research suggests that binaural beats reduce anxiety, depression, and addiction tendencies.

In 2007, *The Journal of Alternative and Complementary Medicine* published a pilot study to assess the psychological and physiological effects of binaural beats. Over a 60-day period, eight adults who suffered from anxiety used binaural beats. The subjects reported a decrease in anxiety and overall increase in the quality of life. An earlier study, conducted by Dr. Arthur Hastings in 1975, showed that binaural beats helped participants fall asleep.

Empaths tend to suffer from anxiety, lack of sleep or disruption in sleep patterns, as well as addictions and depression. Using binaural beats is an excellent tool and exercise that can be used daily to help improve an empath's overall quality of life. Binaural beats can be used during meditation, when taking a nap, or when getting ready to go to sleep for the evening.

Binaural beats can be life changing and I highly recommend incorporating them into your daily life. You can listen to them at the office, while meditating, or when sleeping. As you can see from the studies above, they help with a variety of physical and emotional symptoms that empaths can suffer from.

> **"***Our emotions affect the structure of our DNA, which directly shapes the physical world that we live in every day.***"** —Unknown

CHAPTER FIVE

Empaths and Relationships

Being in a significant relationship (such as with a spouse or partner) can have its challenges. However, certain aspects of relationships with empaths can be more challenging than they are in traditional relationships. Here are 10 things that an empath should keep in mind when engaging in any sort of relationship, especially a romantic one.

1. The empath will always know when something is wrong with their partner. They can tell when their partner is feeling emotions of all kinds, often long before their partner is able to sense their own feelings or troubles. The empath may try to fix issues that haven't even fully risen to the surface yet because the healer in them wants to try to fix or nip whatever is going on in the bud. The partner may not love this. They may feel as if the empath is in their head, invading their privacy.

2. Unlike most people, who have been taught to second-guess their feelings, empaths are very sure about their emotions and can be quick to express them. This can lead to issues for those who are not sure about how they are feeling about decisions or relationship commitments.

3. Empaths can be moody in romantic relationships. Not only does an empath feel their own emotions and energy, they also feel energy and emotions that come at them from all directions. So, if an empath's partner or family member is moody, you can be certain the empath will feel a heightened level of moodiness in response.

4. Empaths crave alone time. It can take an empath a lot of time to decompress, and until they do, there is no way they will be doing anything else. Unfortunately, this can lead to issues if a partner would like to do something with the empath when the empath is trying to decompress.

5. Empaths do not like to give up. Empaths tend to want to hold it together no matter what, so this means that they may try to fix relationships or issues within a relationship that are not fixable. Because empaths are natural healers, they feel a deep frustration if there are hardships in a relationship. If a breakup or divorce happens, you can rest assured that the empath exhausted all resources trying to fix and heal the relationship.

6. Empaths need strong emotional support from their partner. Empaths know that they are "different," and they have felt that way their whole lives, so it is important for them to have a partner who believes in them. Even if they have an idea that may seem crazy, their partner really needs to be supportive.

7. Empaths can feel everything and tend to be very psychic, so an empath's partner better get used to and accept this. It takes a very secure partner to love an empath. An empath's gifts may affect a relationship because the empath is a very loving person who can feel the thoughts and emotions of others. The empath will always want to help and serve. Other people of all kinds will be attracted to the empath. An insecure partner might try to cast their insecurities onto the empath. This can cause the empath to second-guess themselves and hide their light for the sake of keeping the peace and making their partner feel more comfortable.

8. Empaths need the freedom to be who they are. If an empath begins to feel that they are living in a cage, they will want out of the relationship. They cannot handle being controlled.

9. Empaths prefer to sleep alone at times. This gives the empath the opportunity to have uninterrupted time so they can truly rest. The empath's partner may or may not understand this, but hopefully they will. Sometimes, this is the only time the empath will be able to fully get the rest they need.

10. Empaths love to love. They want to share how deeply they feel with their partner in every aspect, especially during sex. Empaths love deeply and crave a soul connection.

In the bedroom, a partner can expect deep connection and long-lasting sex. This time is important to the empath, as they crave an equal energy exchange. The empath's partner should expect and get used to this. On the other hand, it is also important to note that if there has been an argument or emotional upset within the relationship, the empath will have a hard time shutting off any corresponding emotions. As a result, the empath can have a very hard time wanting to be intimate until they get a chance to rebalance and center themselves.

Relationships Between HSPs and Empaths

If an HSP and an empath are in any kind of relationship and they are both hurting or are still learning about their individual, unique sensitivities, it is important to note that they can develop a very codependent relationship. The HSP may constantly seek emotional validation from the empath, and the empath will feel the need to help the HSP heal.

This is not to say that an HSP and an empath cannot have a healthy relationship, as every relationship is unique. However, to allow this to happen, the HSP and the empath would need to set healthy boundaries that allow both individual growth and growth within the relationship. If they are willing to do this, a healthy, balanced relationship can be achieved.

How to Maintain a Healthy Relationship as an Empath

Allow yourself alone time. As an empath, it is essential for you to recharge and get in touch with your unique vibration so you can discern the difference between your feelings and those of your partner. Set aside time every day to reconnect with yourself. If you have to do this daily, then do it. No excuses—you can set aside at least 30 minutes to an hour every day. You are worth the effort. If you are constantly around your partner, how will you ever be able to identify your own vibration and get in touch with your heart space and intuition?

Set healthy boundaries. You need to learn to manage your energy and your partner needs to manage theirs. This way, your relationship's success will not depend on how both of you are feeling moment to moment. It is neither acceptable nor healthy for your partner to purge all of their anxiety onto you. If they are in overwhelm or in fight-or-flight mode, acknowledge that you understand their feelings, but also let them know that the type of energy they are releasing physically and emotionally drains you on a deeper level than they may understand.

Do not give more than you are receiving. If you frequently give your partner support but do not often receive support in return, this causes an energetic imbalance and will quickly wear on you. Allow yourself to receive. A lot of empaths battle with codependent behaviors, and giving more to others for validation tends to be one of these behaviors.

Speak your truth. Be your authentic self, no matter what. Express how you are feeling and expect your feelings to be honored and cherished.

Keep yourself grounded, shielded, and clear. The last thing you or your partner needs is for you to have an energetic blowout. An energetic blowout is when the empath is exhausted and cannot give anymore. Their energy levels are incredibly imbalanced and it may take a few days just to come back online. To avoid a blowout, remember that all of the energy you pick up needs to go somewhere, so it is best to ground it, using practices like meditation, yoga, exercise, Epsom salt baths, or saging (see Chapters 9 and 10). Make sure you take responsibility for staying clear.

Do not allow yourself to take on your partner's energy. As time goes on in the relationship, you will feel and pick up on this person's daily emotions, including frustrations, fears, or worries. Being an empath and the "motherer of others," you will naturally want to fix your partner's burdens or stresses for them. You may think that you are causing these issues or take them on as your own and try to transmute them. This will lead to total exhaustion for you. Let your partner know that you understand what they are going through but that you cannot carry their stresses around for them.

Traits of a Healthy Relationship

Trust. You and your partner trust each other without a doubt. There is never a need to second-guess each other. You simply trust on all levels. In addition, jealousy is not an issue. You're best friends and you adore each other. You both feel whole and have healed any issues around insecurities or jealousy within yourselves.

Honesty. You and your partner can tell each other anything. You allow yourself and your partner to be totally authentic, because you are best friends. It doesn't matter what the truth is; you can tell each other anything and you will still feel unconditional love and admiration.

Independence. You are both whole and independent from one another. You do not need each other for anything; rather, you choose to be in each other's lives.

Equality. You both are considered equals and have equal say in the relationship. One of you does not overpower the other. You choose to openly discuss decisions, and both of your opinions are taken into consideration before a decision is made.

Respect. You and your partner value each other's beliefs and who you are as individual people. You empower each other and encourage one another to be the best versions of yourselves. You do not overstep each other's boundaries.

Loyalty. You and your partner have each other's backs, no matter what. You are both faithful and reliable.

Setting Healthy Boundaries

As an empath, one of the biggest lessons you will be moved through is how to have and maintain healthy boundaries for yourself. If you have little to no boundaries, it is usually a sign of low self-esteem.

Boundaries are essential to maintaining a healthy life and healthy relationships. They are a normal part of life and are necessary. It is important to know this and stand by your boundaries. However, empaths tend to have a very hard time doing this out of fear of saying no or hurting others.

Types of Boundary Violations

Verbal. When another person screams at you, says derogatory comments to you or about you, or says things about you that are untrue as if the comments or statements are true.

Psychological or emotional. When another preys on your self-esteem, demeans you, judges you, manipulates you, tries to embarrass you, shames you, or goes out of their way to make you feel guilty (especially when you have nothing to feel guilty about); when they constantly criticize your thoughts or feelings, or try to convince you that the way they think is superior to your thought process.

Physical. When another invades your personal space, damages or violates your personal property, physically touches or harms you, and otherwise acts inappropriately toward you; this includes inappropriate sexual behavior and violations.

Are you experiencing this? Which of your boundaries are being crossed?

_____

_____

_____

_____

_____

Steps to Help Set Healthy Boundaries

1. Take responsibility for yourself. When you set healthy boundaries for yourself, you are setting an example of how you expect others to treat you.

It is so important to remember that you are ultimately in control. It is up to you to decide how you would like to be treated or what type of energy you allow into your space.

How do you want to be treated?

_____

_____

_____

_____

_____

How do you want to feel?

_____

_____

_____

_____

_____

2. Work on your self-esteem. When you have a healthy respect for yourself and love yourself unconditionally, flaws and all, you will notice that you will spend less time dealing with others who do not respect or cherish you.

This is because you will know that you are worthy of respect and will be able to recognize when another person needs healing that you cannot provide. You can simply choose not to associate with this person.

What are the things you love about yourself?

_____

_____

_____

_____

_____

What talents and gifts do you have?

_____

_____

_____

_____

_____

Building Self-Esteem

Avoid negative self-talk. That inner critic can really keep you from finding balance and achieving what you are worthy of. Instead, say healthy affirmations to yourself every day. See Chapter 9 on chakras for many examples of affirmations.

Stop comparing yourself to others. You are unique and have your own gifts and perspectives. You have your own purpose to fulfill, and it may look very different from someone else's.

Exercise. This is a big one. Get yourself moving and you will feel stronger, healthier, sexier, and more capable of taking on challenges you never thought you could. Personally, I love to run. It is an excellent exercise for burning excess stress and energy.

Do what makes you happy. When we do what we love, we feel naturally better.

Take time to groom. When we feel like we look good, this helps our overall energy and self-confidence. Make the effort to look your best so you can feel your best daily.

---

3. Check the energy of other people. It's important to note how you feel around others. If something feels off when you are around another, there is a reason. Pay attention to your internal radar. If it feels bad to be around someone, stay away. Stay away from anyone who has his or her own agenda, without respect for yours. Vampire energies are a good example of this: An energy vampire is someone who has no problem pushing your limits or taking your energy away.

Provide an example of a person or situation that pushes your limits or takes your energy away.

_____

_____

_____

_____

_____

Set a clear intention of what you will do the next time you are around a person or situation like this.

_____

_____

_____

_____

_____

_____

4. Stop trying to fix everyone. Sometimes, empaths try to fix people because they want to feel loved or validated. This can be a sign of codependency and it is not healthy. When you spend your time trying to fix everyone, it is a waste of energy, because you cannot control the experiences that others choose for themselves. Search deep within yourself as to why you feel that this behavior is necessary.

Why do you feel that you are responsible for fixing people or situations? What type of people or situations do you try to fix?

_____

_____

_____

_____

_____

_____

From whom have you felt a lack of love in your life—parents, siblings, friends, spouse, etc.? In what way?

_____

_____

_____

_____

_____

What has this person(s) triggered in you that needs healing? Has it made you feel insecure, abandoned, rejected?

_____

_____

_____

_____

_____

What are you going to do about it now that you are aware of this wound within you?

_____

_____

_____

_____

_____

_____

5. Walk away. It is okay to change your mind; you don't owe anything to anyone but yourself. Walk away without guilt or fear if you are involved in a situation where you are being treated badly and the other party refuses to change or hear you. You are worthy of an equal energy exchange.

Provide an example of an unhealthy situation or relationship where you are treated unfairly.

_____

_____

_____

_____

_____

_____

What boundaries—verbal, emotional, or physical—are or were being crossed?

_____

_____

_____

_____

_____

Set a clear intention for yourself. How will you address this situation if it happens again?

_____

_____

_____

_____

6. Know yourself. Learn how to separate your beliefs, thoughts, and feelings from those who are around you. Know that it is okay if you feel different from the people you are around daily or were raised around. Often, we are raised with certain types of conditioning or beliefs that keep us from living in alignment with what we are worthy of. For example, conditioned childhood beliefs can keep us from pursuing what we feel is right for us, or projections from parents or family members can interfere with what our hearts truly desire.

What serves me in this moment? What do I truly want? Why am I feeling this way?

_____

_____

_____

_____

_____

What situation or feeling no longer serves me? What do I no longer want? Why am I feeling this way?

_____

_____

_____

_____

_____

Healthy Boundary Affirmations

❖ It's okay to not answer that call

❖ It's okay that I want to speak my mind

❖ It's okay for me to do nothing

❖ It's okay that I desire to be alone

❖ It's okay to change my mind

❖ It's okay to surrender and simply let go

"I allow myself to set healthy boundaries. To say no to what does not align with my values, to say yes to what does. Boundaries assist me to remain healthy, honest, and living a life that is true to me."
　　—Lee Horbachewski

❝*May the next few months be a period of magnificent transformation.*❞
　—Unknown

Energetic Cords and Hooks

As stated before, everything is energy. This includes you. We have an electromagnetic field that surrounds us and interacts with everything we come into contact with. As you become aware of your own energy, it is important to know about energetic cords and hooks. Cords are energetic connections that form between people. They can be good cords formed from positive emotions, such as love, and other times they can be formed from anger, fear, or other negative emotions. Cords are being created consistently and it is important to clear the negative, low-vibration cords that are based in fear.

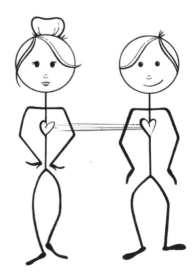

Hooks are formed when other people "hook" into your energy, or vice versa. This happens between two people often, whether they are conscious of it or not. Hooks do not serve you; they are negative and can take away your energy or power. Empaths are often exposed to this type of situation because they are so sympathetic. Hooks are especially likely for empaths who set poor boundaries for themselves, because this causes them to give their power away.

ARE YOU BEING AFFECTED BY UNHEALTHY CORDS AND HOOKS?

1. Do you have a relationship or connection in your life that drains your energy? For example, it's rare, if ever, that you feel good after being around this person. If anything, you feel doubt, guilt, or confusion after you are around them. You may even feel bad about yourself or second-guess your decisions that you felt so clear about before being around them.

If so, provide an example:

_____

_____

_____

_____

_____

_____

2. Do you have someone in your life that projects all of their insecurities onto you? Someone whom you are always trying to make feel better about their issues? Codependent relationships, including those with friends, coworkers, and family members, might look like this. If so, provide an example:

_____

_____

_____

_____

_____

3. Do you have someone in your life whom you are nervous to be your authentic self around, in fear of how they will react? This can often happen with an unsupportive parent, spouse, or family member. They may try to implant their energy into you, keeping you from moving forward and achieving your goals, because your progress makes them feel uncomfortable and forces them to look at their own healing work.

If so, provide an example:

_____

_____

_____

_____

_____

4. Do you have someone in your life who always depends on your energy to make them feel better, asking you to act like a therapist or counselor? For example, when this person calls, you may hesitate to answer the phone but you often do it anyway, because you'll feel bad if you don't.

If so, provide an example:

_____

_____

_____

_____

_____

_____

How to Keep Your Energy Clear

To avoid negative cords and hooks, there's a simple answer: Boundaries, boundaries, and did I mention boundaries? Setting healthy boundaries for yourself is the first essential step for you when it comes to energy management. When you let go of that which does not serve you and make the conscious decision to stop allowing others to drain you of your energy, progress begins.

There are a few other things you can do to protect your energy and remove negative relationships from your life.

Sever cords and remove hooks. You can do this yourself or have this completed by a professional reiki master. I highly recommend having a reiki session every four to six weeks for maintenance (see Chapter 10). If you decide to do this for yourself, here is a little exercise. Imagine yourself being surrounded by white light and ask Archangel Michael to come in and sever any cords that are not serving your highest good. Ask that each cord be released with love and light. If you feel as though you have a hook, which is more deeply ingrained than a cord, ask for assistance on removing the hook, as these need to be removed gently. You can call upon Archangel Raphael to heal the space where the hook sat once it is removed. There are several meditations that you can listen to on YouTube to help assist you with this.

Remember that cords and hooks can come back if you allow them to. So, if you are in a period of learning and transition in your life, it's important to continually practice checking in on your energy.

Stay away from fear-based connections and relationships. Spend time alone to recharge and put yourself first, always. Know that you feel the way you feel for a reason. Love and respect yourself enough to honor your feelings and what your heart and body are trying to tell you.

You will begin to notice a change in yourself when you start removing fear-based cords and hooks in your life. You will feel clearer and more empowered.

You cannot remove a cord that is based in love, so do not worry about this. If there is a cord that you have strung with another that is based in love, it truly can never be severed, no matter how many times you try.

Love vs. Fear in Relationships

Love-Based Relationship	Fear-Based Relationship
Unconditional love and acceptance	At least one partner acts controlling toward the other
Partners are able to communicate about past issues and forgive each other	At least one partner holds onto anger; cannot forgive the other for past mistakes
Both parties trust each other and allow for other types of relationships	At least one partner exhibits jealousy
Both partners support each other and empower each other to be the best version of themselves	Difficulty feeling fulfilled or acting to full capacity
Partners do not manipulate, control, or act with hostility toward each other	Cannot act authentically without upsetting or triggering the other
Partners openly show their love and emotions	At least one partner behaves passive aggressively toward the other
Partners can set and respect each other's boundaries	At least one partner causes the other/suffers from mental or physical abuse
Relationship is based on choice, respect, and communication	Relationship is sustained by a sense of need, not respect
Healthy, heart-based sexual relationship, if applicable	Unhealthy sexual relationship, if applicable

If you are dealing with a fear-based connection in your life, provide an example. What are some patterns or cycles that you recognize? How does it make you feel?

_____

_____

_____

_____

_____

Are you ready to start living in alignment with love? What is your heart telling you? What practical steps do you need to take to align with the vibration of love?

_____

_____

_____

_____

_____

It is important to note that every relationship is different and unique, so it will ultimately be up to you to know if the connection can be healed if it is fear based, or if the cords should be severed forever for the good of both parties.

Energetic Bonds and Links

Now that you know what cords and hooks are, you will now learn how empaths can begin to determine which energy belongs to you and which belongs to another. This is not an easy lesson at all, and it usually takes a lot of hands-on experience (which is not always fun, but is very much necessary) to learn the difference between your energy and that of another.

Empaths are so energetically sensitive that we have the ability to walk into a room and usually know instantly if something is off. If the room is full of heightened anxiety, we feel it. If the room is full of anger or fear and others are trying to hide it, we feel it. This often makes us very anxious. The opposite is also true: When we are around others who are full of positivity, calmness, and love, we feel it and soak it up like a sponge. It may be hard at first to tell whether you are feeling your own energy or someone else's. These are a few examples of what picking up on another person's energy might look like or feel like:

- Feeling bombarded with memories involving a person, or not being able to get them off of your mind. This is usually an indicator that this person is thinking of you and, likewise, cannot get you off of their mind.

- Wanting to contact a person right away, even though you don't understand why.

- Feeling sexual energy toward a person or coming from a person. A lot of intuitive empaths can feel when someone is directing sexual energy toward them or having an intimate moment with another.

- Having very detailed dreams about a person, in which they deliver messages to you or messages are received about what is going on or about to go on in their life.

- Panicking or stressing about issues that you have already worked through. For example: You have already been moved through a lesson, have accepted the teaching, and have grown from it. But, at 2 a.m., you wake up in tears feeling like you must process what you cleared months ago. This may happen because the other person involved in the lesson is remembering you or having a painful heart-opening experience due to the strength and growth that you are reflecting back at them. If you are on a twin flame journey (see page 68), this can be one of the most annoying things to deal with. It is so important to remember that this is not you.

Have you experienced or are you currently experiencing anything like the examples above? Provide an example:

_____

_____

_____

_____

_____

_____

_____

Types of Energetic Connections

We establish bonds and connections with many people throughout our journey—for example, family, friends, those whom we consider to be soul family. As an empath, it is important for you to know that due to your beautiful ability to feel even the most subtle of energies, there will be times when you will feel an emotion that may come directly from one of these connections in your life. Although it may feel like it is yours, it isn't. You are simply picking up on this other person's energy. They may be going through something internally or directly thinking about and projecting energy onto you. Either way, whether it is positive or negative energy, you will feel it.

If you want to understand what it means to have an energetic connection with someone, think about the empathic bond between a mother and her child. This same type of energetic connection is formed between empaths and their soulmates, and for those of you who are on a twin flame self-mastery journey, between you and your counterpart.

Once an energetic connection is established by a strong emotion, it is not easily broken. A bond that is formed by love will never go away. That connection will always be there. There are many types of soulmates that an empath may encounter; here are a few.

Soul family. This can be immediate family or those whom we consider to be our soul family. Soul family members are together to support each other and learn lessons together and from one another. These family members help one another to grow from whatever they all need to master in this life.

Karmic teacher soulmate. This is a significant relationship, friendly or romantic, that teaches us vital lessons we need to learn for and about ourselves. Karmic teacher soulmates will bring out the best and the worst in you. These relationships are formed from a deep soul connection and can be very painful when the lessons are completed. Often, these connections are extremely fear-based or codependent.

Life-partner soulmate. The soulmate with whom you spend the rest of your life. This is typically a love-based relationship.

Romantic soulmate. A romantic soulmate connection usually runs smoothly, and there are no obstacles to this type of connection because it holds a purpose that will serve both parties involved. Both souls involved in these types of connections agree to learn something from one another, and this agreement, or soul contract, must be experienced by both parties, either consciously or unconsciously, for their highest good and optimum soul growth.

Twin souls/Twin flames. This person is the mirror of your soul. A twin flame is a person who you feel connected to in all ways—physically, emotionally, and spiritually. This type of sacred connection is based in unconditional love and will cause growth and total transformation of the soul.

A twin flame connection is a difficult connection to have, because both parties have so much healing and growth to do. Both parties must come into sacred union with themselves, unifying the feminine and masculine energy within and come into wholeness, which can take years. These connections are truly spiritual because they encourage each party to grow and break down old patterns so they live in direct alignment with love. Doing so is difficult for a single person to do, and it can be especially challenging for two people who are energetically connected to do so simultaneously.

No matter how hard you try to not feel your twin's energy, it happens anyway, especially if they are experiencing some serious soul lessons and growth. Not every empath is going to be on a twin flame journey. However, many people who find themselves on a twin flame journey are incredibly psychic and beautiful empaths with a lot of gifts. I have been blessed to meet quite a few of them. Having a twin will be one way that you will learn that separation is truly an illusion.

A twin flame connection will force you and your twin to drop barriers and learn about unconditional love. If your twin has come into your life, this means you are ready to grow. This is a bond that is formed through quantum entanglement, a phenomenon in which particles affect each other instantaneously across any type of distance. Particles that are connected will remain connected at even the farthest distance: at opposite sides of the country, world, or even universe. This type of connection will lead you down the fast track to the path of ascension, which you will learn more about in Chapter 7.

> Whoever you feel strongly toward, whether positively or negatively, they are most likely a soulmate who is here to teach you something for your soul's growth.

RETURNING ANOTHER'S ENERGY

Double check and really see if the energy you are feeling is really yours or not. If you were feeling just fine and then this energy hits you, odds are, this is not yours.

Take a deep breath, ground yourself, and visualize blowing the energy back toward your energetic connection. I recommend saying "that is not mine, that is yours to feel" out loud.

You can also complete the above exercise if you are being bombarded by low vibrational energy from others while out and about or at work. If someone is overwhelming you with energy, just take a deep breath and blow the energy lightly back toward them. If they are in your face or standing too close, imagine doing this in your head. It sounds weird, but it totally works.

Intimate Relationships and Energy

When it comes to intimate relationships, it is important to always be mindful of whom you share your energy with. Think of sex as a sacred energy exchange. Being an empath, you will absorb what another person is carrying around with them on a deeper level, and if it is not an equal energy exchange, you do not want it. If the person that you are choosing to share your energy with is full of anxiety, worry, fear, or doubt, you can guarantee this is the energy that you will absorb and continue to feel and carry with you until it is cleared.

Everything is energy, and anything that is communicated between two people is a simple energetic exchange. Sex is the most powerful exchange we can share with another, so it is important to be mindful with whom you share your sacred energy.

When you sleep with someone, no matter how insignificant you may think it was, it leaves what could be called energetic debris. You will feel and carry the energy of those with whom you have been intimate, and this energy can stay with you for a long period of time. The more you intimately interact with another person, the deeper the connection and the more their electromagnetic field is meshed with yours. So if this person constantly lives in a place of fear or has slept with a lot of people who live in a place of lower vibrational energy, you will begin to pick up this vibration, carry it, and emit it, as well.

It is very important to exchange your sacred energy with someone who provides a love-based energy equal to yours, because when two people have sex with pure, intentional love and adoration, the heart opens and the energy that is exchanged can literally heal one another. DNA can activate and unlock, both parties will be able to align with their higher selves, and the energy exchanged can help transmute emotional trauma. When this type of energy is exchanged, it will feel replenishing.

> **"***If you knew just how powerful sex is, you would never have it with just anyone ever again.***"** —Unknown

Achieving Balance in Relationships

We each have masculine and feminine energy within us. It is crucial that we are in balance with both of these energies within ourselves if we desire to be in a sacred relationship with another. We are entering a new paradigm where we are saying goodbye to the old patriarchal ways of force and control and we are honoring the feminine way of feeling and flowing.

So how do we do this? Let's start with understanding feminine energy and masculine energy.

Feminine Energy Traits
Receiving
Feeling
Intuitive
Creative
Flowing
Loving
Allows pursuit

Masculine Energy Traits
Giving
Thinking
Analytical
Active
Forceful
Mindful
Pursues

How do these two energies play out within an individual? It's about allowing the heart-based feminine energy to lead you. Allow yourself to feel first before you do anything, then once you have clarity on what your feelings are trying to communicate, take action based on what your heart wants to achieve or experience.

One must find balance between the two energies; if the energies are unbalanced in either direction, that can also cause problems.

Unbalanced Energy

Too Much Feminine Energy
Lack of structure and focus
Difficulty making decisions—it can take days, or even years, to decide
Hard time focusing on or accomplishing basic tasks
Overreliance on emotion, without taking action
Disorganized
Low self-esteem

Too Much Masculine Energy
Sticks to routines and patterns that may not be fulfilling
Risk-averse and afraid of new opportunities
Controlling of both outcomes and people
Overreliance on logic and analysis; unable to let the heart guide
Difficulty living in the moment
Overly critical

The individual who can balance the sacred feminine and sacred masculine within themselves is truly empowered and will be able to create whatever reality they desire. The balanced individual will not require validation from anyone. They will feel whole within. This will ultimately add value to their partner's life, as well.

Do you feel like you are living too much in your feminine energy or your masculine energy? How can you achieve more balance?

_____

_____

_____

_____

_____

“ *The sacred union of feminine and masculine energies within the individual is the basis of all creation.* ” —Shakti Gawain

Energy Vampires

As an empath, it's likely that at some time in your life, you will encounter an energy vampire. Energy vampires are individuals who are not yet mature enough to handle their own emotions. They often feel as though the whole world revolves around them and they have a hard time seeing anything from another person's point of view.

Energy vampires will suck the energy right out of an empath and not think twice about it because they typically lack empathy. They have allowed their vibration to drop so low that they unfortunately have the need to feed off of other people's energy. They are takers, not givers.

An energy vampire holds onto a lot of resentment and complains constantly. They will have aggressive or passive-aggressive tendencies, and will gossip about others frequently, picking apart the actions of others while refusing to take responsibility for themselves. Energy vampires love to argue, debate, or pick fights with others. They always crave the need to be right and can engage in manipulative behavior, such as guilt tripping. At the same time, they tend to hold a victim mentality, and may have narcissistic traits.

You may feel or experience the following symptoms when around an energy vampire:

◆ Overwhelm and exhaustion

◆ Stress

◆ Anxiety

◆ Body pain

◆ Headaches

◆ The desire to run away

How to Protect Your Energy

Since emotional vampires feed off of the reaction of others, it is important to not give in to their desire to get a heightened reaction out of you. Make the conscious decision to stay calm around this person. Always remain neutral and certainly never argue with an emotional vampire. If you choose to engage with them, this will ultimately feed them and drain you.

Spend as little time with an emotional vampire as possible. It can also be beneficial to have a buffer of some kind to help manage the emotional vampire. For example, if you know you are going to be around someone who drains you, balance the situation by bringing someone that lifts you and helps raise your vibration.

Visualize a protective shield or buffer between you and the emotional vampire. I use a little technique where I imagine white light coming out from the center of my chest and expanding like a bubble all around my body. I expand the bubble a few inches around me. If I still feel overwhelm or exhaustion, I will repeat this process and then take a deep breath and blow away any energy that is not serving me. Think of it as filtering yourself.

Do you have an emotional vampire in your life? Provide an example or write an affirmation for yourself to remind you of how important your time and energy truly is.

_____

_____

_____

_____

_____

_____

_____

Protection Affirmation

I honor and respect myself enough not to allow others to control, manipulate, or dominate me in any way. I will only allow my energy to be used in a way that serves me positively.

" *The less you respond to negative people, the more peaceful your life will become.* " —Unknown

Codependency

Empaths are susceptible to unhealthy codependent behaviors and relationships. It is important to note that we are all codependent (seeking validation from others) on some level, and even the healthiest relationships have some codependency in them.

In healthy, giving relationships, both parties rely on each other in healthy ways. The people in the relationship are stronger together than they are apart and they bring out the best in each other. Both parties in the relationship benefit from the connection and it is not parasitic.

Codependency becomes unhealthy when one party feeds off the other in a destructive way. The relationship is dysfunctional and enables bad habits, addictions, immaturity, poor mental health, or low self-worth in one or both parties. Many empaths find themselves in codependent relationships because they are natural healers and use the relationship to validate themselves in some way, or will find themselves trying to "fix" the other person. Every case is different, but this usually has to do with a wounded inner child within the empath.

Take the following quiz to see if you are codependent.

QUIZ: ARE YOU CODEPENDENT?

1. Do you give until your cup is totally empty?   ○ YES   ○ NO

2. Do you place the wants and needs of others before your own?   ○ YES   ○ NO

3. Do you enable the destructive behavior of others in order to avoid a conflict?   ○ YES   ○ NO

4. Do you have a hard time setting boundaries with others?   ○ YES   ○ NO

5. Do you value the approval of others more than you value yourself?   ○ YES   ○ NO

6. Do you suffer from fears of abandonment or rejection?   ○ YES   ○ NO

7. Do you have a hard time making decisions? When you do finally make a decision, do you constantly second-guess yourself?   ○ YES   ○ NO

8. If you are in a relationship, do you find yourself putting all of your focus on the other person? For example, do you make their happiness your top priority, sometimes dismissing your own feelings?   ○ YES   ○ NO

9. Do you take on the pain, struggles, stress, and worries of others, often making it a priority to fix these issues for them? Do you feel as though you need to "rescue" others?   ○ YES   ○ NO

10. Do you feel guilty for saying no?   ○ YES   ○ NO

If you answered "Yes" to more than five of these questions, you are likely in a codependent relationship.

Provide an example or situation in your life where you may be giving your power away.

What needs to change in order to claim back your power?

_____

_____

_____

_____

_____

_____

_____

Are you willing to make this change so you can become a stronger, more capable version of you?

◯ YES   ◯ NO

What are your next action steps?

_____

_____

_____

_____

_____

_____

_____

How to Avoid Unhealthy Codependent Relationships

Start by setting an intention. Ask yourself what you desire from your relationships, either platonic or romantic. Dig deep here. Take the time to visualize yourself in a healthy and loving relationship where the energy exchange taking place is equal. I often suggest to my clients to write down a list of everything they desire out of a partner and post it up somewhere they see it daily.

Allow yourself to receive and drop the barriers. More often than not, we ask the universe for what we want and then we block it from coming in due to our attachments, expectations on how it will come, or fear of not getting what we want. Set clear intentions by listening to your heart and then allow what comes into your life to come and allow what goes out of your life to go. It is all happening for a reason.

Then, when starting a relationship, take the time to notice all the red flags. Often, a codependent partner or "friend" is jealous, insecure, possessive, and controlling. If you notice anything like this, nip it in the bud as fast as you can, or move on. You should not feel as though you are walking on eggshells around a friend or partner. If this is the case, this person has a lot of inner wounding and healing to face before they can ever be a healthy, giving person.

Remember, you are worthy of abundance on every level. You deserve an equal exchange of energy in every aspect of your life and in every relationship. Accept balance and do not give more than you get from any connection in your life. Believe in yourself and know that you are deserving of love. No matter what. Be compassionate toward yourself. Remember, we typically attract what we have not healed yet until we do, so keep working on yourself and keep that self-esteem and vibration high!

> **"***We get to decide who we allow into our inner sanctum. Not everyone deserves an all-access pass.***"** —Kris Carr

HOW TO IDENTIFY AN UNHEALTHY CODEPENDENT RELATIONSHIP

First, be honest with yourself. I have found that often people who are in unhealthy relationships dismiss or forget what they are experiencing on a daily basis. Having physical notes and examples helps with a perspective shift if needed.

In your relationship, are there more bad days than good days? If you are not sure, take a moment over the next week or so to check in. For each day this week, circle whether the day was good or bad.

Monday	Good or Bad		Friday	Good or Bad
Tuesday	Good or Bad		Saturday	Good or Bad
Wednesday	Good or Bad		Sunday	Good or Bad
Thursday	Good or Bad			

Write about both the good and bad days below. What was specifically bad about the bad days? What was specifically good about the good days?

_____

_____

_____

_____

_____

_____

How many days were good? _____

How many days were bad? _____

Repeat this exercise for a few weeks to see if you notice a visual pattern that is cycling. If so, consult with your team and make a plan to leave the relationship.

Leaving a toxic relationship is never easy, especially the more entangled you may be. However, the more true you are to your emotions, the closer emotional freedom is.

"*You owe yourself the love you so lovingly give to other people.*" —Unknown

CHAPTER SIX

Specific Challenges for Empaths

Because empaths are so energetically sensitive, an empath can suffer from one or more of the symptoms listed in this chapter. I've included tips for how to handle each of the symptoms listed. For more advice on dealing with everyday challenges, revisit the Are You an Empath? quiz on page 9.

Odd Sleep Patterns and Insomnia

Many empaths have problems falling asleep, and then they will have issues staying asleep. This is especially true around new and full moons, if they are having a hard time listening to their intuition, when they are picking up on a partner's or family member's energy, or if there is something they may be picking up from the collective consciousness. For example, empaths can, and usually will, feel anxiety or nervousness when there is a major disaster.

On the other hand, it is also very common for empaths to get a lot done or step into their creativity very late at night. This is usually because they can tune in very easily to their own vibration without interruption. Empaths may feel drained during the day and then all of a sudden get a massive spark of energy late in the evening, which leads them to complete a whole project by morning.

If you are an empath and, like most of the population, cannot stay up until all hours of the evening due to work and family schedules, I highly suggest setting up a regular workout routine to help burn and process the excess energy you have absorbed throughout the day, which is what keeps you stimulated. It is amazing what 30 minutes to an hour of exercise can do. On my own journey, this is something I have had to learn to incorporate often. If I don't, I can literally be up all night long. I also recommend doing evening meditation, 20 to 30 minutes before bedtime. This will help calm you and prepare the mind for sleep.

Adrenal Fatigue

I have worked with many empaths who suffer from adrenal fatigue. Adrenal fatigue is a collection of symptoms like insomnia, body aches, and pain, as well as total and complete exhaustion. Even if the empath has slept for many hours, the empath will still feel tired.

Adrenal fatigue seems to cause controversy among different medical professionals, but it is caused by high levels of stress, which is very harsh on the adrenal glands. During adrenal fatigue, the adrenal glands are unable to keep up the pace with the demands of fight-or-flight stimulation. In other words, your body believes it is constantly in danger, even when it isn't, and it starts to wear itself out. Overworking the adrenal glands can result in erratic spikes of the stress hormone cortisol, even when it is not needed. When the body is so busy producing cortisol, it cannot make other important hormones like aldosterone, testosterone, and epinephrine, which are much needed for managing stress. This can eventually lead to a burnout, characterized by exhaustion and depression.

Symptoms of having high levels of cortisol include:

- Poor sleep quality
- High blood pressure
- Thyroid issues

- Anxiety or depression
- Weight gain
- Excess belly fat

Thyroid Issues

I have met a lot of empaths who seem to have a problem with their thyroid. Even though there are no medical studies claiming that thyroid issues and being an empath are directly connected, I can usually pick up on this issue with many empaths as soon as I am working on their throat chakra during a reiki session. The thyroid is associated with the throat chakra (see page 130).

It seems the throat chakra, and thus the thyroid, is very unbalanced for many empaths who have had a hard time speaking their soul's truth, or who have had their voice dismissed or suppressed for a long time. It's important to remember that anything that is not healed from within will manifest itself in the physical body. If you are a female empath, irregular menstrual cycles that can lead to extreme pain or heavy bleeding can be a sign that your thyroid is out of balance. This is connected to the sacral chakra, which can symbolize suppression of your intuition and feminine energy.

Sensitivities to Chemicals

Empaths and HSPs tend to be very sensitive to chemicals such as harsh cleaners, dyes, and perfumes. They can be very hard on an empath and will often send them into a sneezing frenzy or give them a headache. You may find yourself naturally drawn to cleaning with natural or organic products.

Maintaining a Healthy Diet

Because an empath's energy levels can become depleted rather quickly throughout the day, it is important to incorporate high vibrational/high energy food into the diet, like organic vegetables and fruits. These foods are considered high energy because they have not been processed; they are pure.

Many empaths, at one point or another on their journey, find themselves completely overhauling their diet and may end up going vegetarian or vegan. If you do this, make sure you are getting the right amount of nutrients.

The key is to be conscious about what makes you feel good when you eat it. Incorporating the right mixture of fresh food into a daily diet will help the empath replenish energy more effectively and quickly.

Supplements and Mineral Deficiencies

Empaths and healers benefit greatly from taking minerals and supplements. In fact, it wasn't until I was on my path of becoming an intuitive healer that I realized just how important and essential these things were for my health and wellbeing.

Because empaths pick up on the energy of others, our energy levels are depleted faster. It is crucial for us to keep our health up so we can move through life more easily.

You will notice a difference in your energy levels or patterns when you incorporate vitamins and supplements from the following list into your daily routine, in addition to maintaining a healthy diet. However, please remember: Only you know your body and it is important to do your research or talk with a medical professional for your own personal needs.

- L-Theanine: Helps maintain a sense of overall calm

- Magnesium: A calming and relaxing mineral, this can be taken orally or through Epsom salt baths.

- Selenium: Helps the everyday function of the thyroid

- Vitamin B: Helps with energy levels

- Vitamin C: Helps with energy levels

- Vitamin D: Helps with serotonin levels

- Holy Basil (Tulsi): Helps with energy levels (a personal favorite of mine; often consumed as tea)

- Ashwagandha: Supports the endocrine system, supports adrenal fatigue, and can promote a sense of calm.

Emotional Eating

Empaths may find themselves eating for no other reason than to have a little bit of immediate comfort when they feel especially sensitive and overwhelmed by negative vibrations. Basically, something is being triggered within the empath and causing stress, so they resort to a quick fix. By overeating, some empaths seek to create a "barrier" of excess weight to protect themselves from absorbing the subtle (or sometimes very harsh) energies around them. This is especially true when an empath is experiencing and being moved through their own stressful life lessons or situations.

I have worked with many empaths and there is not one who doesn't crave carbs or a combination of sugar and salts when they are not grounded or when they are having a hard time dealing with excessive energy. Let's discuss a couple of the common triggers that are directly connected to empaths overeating.

Stress and anxiety. When an empath is in fight-or-flight mode, the body has a reaction that causes the hypothalamus to produce corticotropin. This means that it shuts down the appetite. However, when an individual is living in a chronic state of stress, the body begins to react differently and starts producing cortisol, which promotes an appetite increase. See more about adrenal fatigue and chronic stress on page 82.

To help combat stress and anxiety, pinpoint and alleviate the chronic stress in your lifestyle and be true to your emotions. This will help you lose the urge to overeat.

Lack of sleep. When we do not get the proper amount of sleep, the body overproduces ghrelin, also known as the "hunger hormone." Numerous studies have shown that individuals who get less than seven or eight hours of sleep each night are more prone to be overweight.

As discussed previously, exercise will help an empath shed any excess energy that they have absorbed throughout the day. Meditation before bedtime, specifically meditation focused on the third eye, can help relax the empath and help with melatonin release. These practices will help with sleep, which can help reduce appetite.

Lack of grounding. Food is a connection to the physical world. Since empaths can struggle with being grounded, often feeling like they are "out of their body" and disconnected, they naturally want to go do something that counteracts this overwhelming feeling and causes them to feel more grounded. Food is often the quickest solution, because carbs and heavier foods make us feel weighted and full. When we feel full, we slow down and feel more grounded and comfortable.

To avoid overeating but still feel grounded, you can practice grounding exercises daily, such as walking barefoot on the earth for at least five minutes a day, doing physical activity, using essential oils, and doing meditation. For more, see Chapter 10: Tools for Empaths.

Physical Health

Empaths are often people pleasers or diffusers of situations. They will often do whatever they can to keep the peace with and between others to avoid being exposed to negative or harsh energy. Unfortunately, this is done at their own expense and can lead to the empath suffering in silence. Empaths often ignore their own physical and emotional pain to put others first. For example:

- taking care of the mental and physical needs of others before themselves

- making sure another is feeling calm or worry free, even when personally stressed

- doing something for another person even when completely exhausted

Most people are quick to discuss what is bothering them with other people, but an empath will usually not do this. Empaths are known to carry any burdens (emotional or physical) they may be feeling within and try to tackle the issue alone rather than share it with another. They will simply ignore their own burdens or ailments until the issue gets loud enough that they are pretty much forced to deal with it.

Take time for you. Instead of bottling up your emotions or letting your pains develop, allow yourself decompression time daily and time to treat your own wounds. You cannot help others if your energy is low and you are trying to pour from an empty cup. Rest, go for a walk, read, meditate, go to a yoga class—do whatever resonates with you and helps you find balance.

Express your needs. It's also important to learn to say NO and lose the guilt around saying it. "No" is actually a complete sentence. Express yourself to others. If there are people, places, or situations that are not serving you, speak up about it and let others know how you are feeling. This gives the opportunity for change; if the situation still does not change, it is time for a reassessment and possible release.

Listen to your body. The body often expresses to us when something is wrong both physically and emotionally. If something feels off, it's because something usually is. According to Louise L. Hay, author of *Heal Your Body A–Z*, there is a reason for pain in specific areas of the body, described in the chart below.

Body Pain and Associated Conditions

Pain Location	Association
Neck	Stubbornness and inflexibility; refusing to see other points of view
Shoulder	Attitude toward life; ability to live with joy
Upper back	Lack of emotional support; holding back love
Mid-back	Guilt
Lower back	Fear of lack; financial and material support
Elbow	Change and new experiences
Wrist	Ease of movement
Hip	Fear of forward progress, big decisions; feeling that there is nothing to look forward to in life
Knee	Ego and pride; stubbornness and fear
Ankle	Ability to receive pleasure
Foot/bunions	Lack of joy

Addictive Behaviors

Because an empath is usually processing so much within, they often resort to addictive behaviors to help calm or numb them. An unbalanced or unaware empath can get to the point where they simply do not want to feel anymore. To avoid falling into addictive patterns, focus on becoming grounded and cultivating a healthy mental state. Many of the other tips in this chapter can help you avoid addictive behaviors.

Common addictive behaviors include:

- ◆ Excessive eating
- ◆ Alcohol consumption
- ◆ Using drugs
- ◆ Overspending
- ◆ Smoking

Alcohol, drugs, or food can shift an empath's vibration higher or lower. This can stop the empath from feeling energetically sensitive, which of course, can become addictive when you are not wanting to feel so much all of the time. If you do fall into an addictive pattern, seek help from your team and caring professionals.

Mental Health

Because empaths are so keenly tuned in to the world around them, they are likely to experience stress and anxiety. We're going to specifically talk about how empaths can handle low self-esteem, problems with self-esteem, living in the moment, and feeling misunderstood.

Self-Esteem and Self-Worth

Empaths naturally have very big hearts and can have a hard time with situations and people in their lives that are not serving them. However, because of our caring nature, we often feel bad for those who are actually harming us. We feel as if we can heal a person or situation, even when it is not serving us. A disempowered empath may set boundaries that are healthy for them but later feel bad for setting them.

To solve this problem, bring the focus back to yourself. Know that your energy levels matter and every time you interact with another person, whether through phone calls, texts, or in person, you are literally giving a little bit of your energy away.

So, if needed, ask yourself daily, "what is serving me and what is not?" If you know that there is a situation in your life that is not serving you but you go back and interact with it again and again, in the same manner, without change, it is a self-worth issue.

Exercise and finding a like-minded group of individuals are both good ways to improve your self-esteem. Focusing on your solar plexus chakra is a good way to help with your self-worth and self-esteem. See page 126 to learn about daily affirmations and solar plexus meditation, and page 120 to learn the Breath of Fire Technique.

Overthinking and Worrying

As empaths, we feel everything. Unfortunately, this can lead an empath to go into overthinking and worry mode. When an empath feels new energy, they may wonder why it is happening, if it is theirs, what it means, and what is going to happen next, and then they may worry that if they do something or make a wrong decision, it will change an outcome for them that is not in their favor. All of those thoughts can run through an empath's mind within seconds.

It's crucial for empaths to become aware of their thought patterns. When we are not aware of our patterns, we create them again and again. So, any time you find yourself in an anxious situation or having a negative thought, take a step backward and say to yourself, "It is okay that I had that thought, but now I am going to replace it with a positive thought."

Stop focusing so much on what could go wrong and start focusing more on what could go right. We can prevent ourselves from forward movement when we focus on and give our power away to fear. Doing this sends us in a downward spiral.

Try these practices to learn to focus on your thought patterns:

Meditation. This may seem to be the answer for a lot of the issues presented; that's because it helps. Meditation can bring us back into the moment and stop us from overanalyzing the future. I recommend root chakra meditations for this (page 123).

Practice gratitude daily. Spend time every day thinking about everything that you are grateful for. The new opportunities, the release, the daily blessings you have—all of it. This will help shift you into abundance consciousness instead of focusing on lack or worry.

Take a moment to list five things you are grateful for now:

_____

_____

_____

_____

_____

Have a short worry session. Cap your overthinking and worrying session at 15 minutes. It's okay to feel all that you are feeling, but how is dwelling on it going to fix it? Literally give yourself a timer if you need to. Once the timer goes off, go do something fun, get out of the house, and allow yourself to receive an energy shift.

Difficulty Living in the Moment

Especially for intuitive empaths who may know what is coming up for them, it can be very difficult to live in the here and now. The empath can sense subtle shifts and feel the possibility of something happening, which causes them to have a hard time living in the moment. Try a few of the tips below to help ground yourself and live in the moment.

Accept where you are at right now. This moment is all we truly have; we have the free will to do with it what we may. We can choose to put our energy toward fear or we can choose to put our energy toward love. Accepting where we are at the moment doesn't mean that we have arrived at our final destination; it just means we are choosing to work with what we have.

Surrender the illusion of control. Stop trying to control outcomes. Practice detachment from how you think things should be and allow the energy of flow to create miracles for you. Use daily affirmations to help with this:

I am exactly where I am meant to be in this moment in time

I release the past

I release the need to know how it's all going to work out

I release the fear of the unknown

In this moment, I feel peaceful and content

Feeling Totally Misunderstood

Empaths do not usually enjoy "normal conversations" or small talk of any kind. An empath usually wants to go into deep, thought-provoking topics that lead them to a discussion for hours. We want to talk about love, energy, soul bonds, outer space, why we are here, and more. We usually have a very strong intuitive understanding about these topics.

If an empath feels uncomfortable or like they will be attacked for the way they feel, they will most likely hide their feelings from others. Empaths are excellent at this when they feel the need to guard themselves. More often than not, the empath will be titled as "different" or "too emotional" by others.

One of the biggest things I wish I would've known when I was younger is that not everyone is going to see things from a higher perspective. Do yourself a favor now and lose the people-pleasing or validation-seeking attitude. There is no need to explain yourself to everyone.

Empaths are beautiful and unique souls who hold wisdom that not everyone will be able to comprehend, so at times, you may experience the fear-based energy of others. It's okay. Send these people love and light, accept where they are on their journey, and move forward. Here are two other tips to embrace:

Find your tribe. It's crucial to surround yourself with supportive, like-minded individuals. There is nothing better than being able to connect with others and have authentic and compassionate relationships in your life. Join a meditation group, yoga studio, or creative space, or go on a spiritual retreat to find your tribe. Whatever resonates best with you!

Accept who you are. Because empaths can be such people pleasers, it's important to maintain a healthy understanding of yourself. Otherwise, you can get lost in who and what it is that other people want you to be. Know thyself and if others cannot see your light and accept you for exactly who you are, that is their internal healing issue, not yours.

Discernment

Discernment is the ability to judge well. Learning discernment and good judgment is a vital lesson for empaths on their journey, one I have spoken with many of my clients and followers about.

Many empaths have experienced relationships, either in childhood or later in life, where they were told that they couldn't trust their feelings and were discouraged or often scolded for expressing what they felt. They were taught fear and codependency instead of wholeness.

It is vital as an empath to only look within for validation. You do not need anyone else to validate what you are feeling. You feel the way you do for a reason. Once you begin to trust in your recurring feelings, doubt fades. Your sensitivity and intuitive gifts grow stronger, and you will begin to feel more capable and empowered.

> **"**Discernment is the capacity to identify the difference between what is truth and what is illusion, or a lie, or just the result of chaotic thinking.**"**
> —Caroline Myss

CHAPTER SEVEN

Evolving as an Empath

Humanity has been living in a very patriarchal society for thousands of years. We are very much driven by the masculine energy of control, which forces us to align with whatever the mind tells us is logical and causes us to suppress the ancient wisdom that is held within our hearts. We have been encouraged for far too long to listen to our heads instead of our hearts.

I have heard many people over the years make comments about how "they wished that life came with instructions," and I'd like to take a moment to remind the beautiful soul reading this that it does. Our emotions are the map. We are born with a blueprint inside of our hearts that leads us every step of the way, as long as we are willing to trust in and honor our emotions.

When we are in alignment with what is meant for us, we are happy. When we are not in alignment with what is meant for us, we are not happy. If we are sad, angry, worried, or unfulfilled, it is a powerful indicator that something needs to change in order for us to come back into balance with the vibration of love.

Awakening

Spiritual ascension, also known as a spiritual awakening, is a process of shedding the old version of oneself, ultimately leading one to experiencing a total rebirth. It's a complete and total transformation of the soul. Ascension is the acceleration of vibrational energy and the expansion of awareness, which ultimately creates a shift in consciousness for the person being moved through this experience.

When you experience spiritual ascension, you are slowly removing everything within you that is fear based and not true to the vibration of love. Accomplishing this requires relinquishing and purging the patterns of living in alignment with fear. Old patterns will begin to fall away as you embody more light. When moving through ascension, you are merging with your higher self, opening your heart, moving toward your full authenticity. To ascend is to realign with divine love.

Moving through a purification of the soul is certainly not all sunshine, enlightenment, and rainbows. Sure, you'll receive downloads, beautiful insights, clarity, and epiphanies. However, the ascension process comes with all kinds of side effects, such as facing all of your feelings, purging of your ego, facing your darkest fears, and working on issues of codependency so you can ultimately come back to a place of wholeness and sacred union. Essentially, this is a spiritual cleansing.

Many people being moved through an awakening process will be up late into the evening or wake up at odd times of the night experiencing intense emotions or thought processing.

Does this sound like something you are being moved through? In the following quiz, you will find 15 signs and symptoms of awakening/ascension. It is important to note that the ascension process is different for everyone and symptoms can vary for each individual. I personally had a cough that was so bad, it lasted me about two months when I was being guided to speak my truth and come out publicly as an intuitive psychic empath. It was absolutely awful, but the energy block that was held there for so long needed to be cleared.

It's important to note that by releasing suppressed lower vibrational energy such as pain, guilt, or grief that has been weighing you down, you become free to awaken and to ascend. Once this healing is completed and released, you become stronger and more capable to share your own unique divine light, which moves you forward on your path.

QUIZ: ARE YOU BEING MOVED THROUGH ASCENSION?

1. You just know that something is changing; you may not be able to put your finger on it just yet. Old unresolved hurts and pains may be coming up for resolution and clearing. ○ YES ○ NO

2. You are experiencing a lot of strange "coincidences" and synchronicity at a rapid rate. ○ YES ○ NO

3. You are experiencing cold- or flu-like symptoms that seem to last forever. ○ YES ○ NO

4. You are experiencing headaches, body aches, and so much fatigue. You struggle to even get going, and no matter what you do, you cannot seem to get enough rest or sleep. ○ YES ○ NO

5. You are experiencing tingling in the hands or top of the head. Sometimes it can feel like someone is playing with your hair or ants are crawling on your hands. This sensation really increases when you meditate. ○ YES ○ NO

6. You are experiencing changes in vision or perception. You may be seeing glimpses of shadows, flashes of light, sparkles, colors, and energy around others. Sometimes your eyes feel heavy or like they are having a hard time adjusting throughout the day. ○ YES ○ NO

7. Your diet is changing. You may be feeling the need to stop eating meat, or more drawn toward higher vibrational foods such as fruits and vegetables.

◯ YES   ◯ NO

8. You are experiencing a total change in sleep patterns, and possibly periods of restlessness, insomnia, or sporadic sleep schedules.

◯ YES   ◯ NO

9. You are experiencing inexplicable nervousness or anxiety that comes and goes. It feels like a surge of energy and you cannot seem to ground yourself.

◯ YES   ◯ NO

10. You are experiencing a need to love yourself more. You see that you have not been true to yourself or what your heart has been saying, and have possibly been settling for less than you are worthy of.

◯ YES   ◯ NO

11. You desire to be alone more.

◯ YES   ◯ NO

12. You feel like you have lost your identity and you are trying to find your true self or purpose. You may feel like you have a mission or special purpose you are meant to fulfill.

◯ YES   ◯ NO

13. You are losing track of time and lack focus.

◯ YES   ◯ NO

14. You are feeling overwhelming feelings of love and are coming into an understanding that we are all one and everything is connected.

◯ YES   ◯ NO

15. You are experiencing an increase in psychic gifts or experiences such as clairvoyance, clairaudience, claircognizance, and clairsentience. Your intuition and sensitivities are getting stronger in general.

○ YES   ○ NO

If you answered yes to seven or more of those questions, you are most likely being moved through an ascension/spiritual awakening.

Take a moment to write down some of your experiences here, but also make sure you are keeping a journal of all that you are feeling, sensing, seeing, and hearing.

_____

_____

_____

_____

_____

_____

_____

" *Go easy on yourself, you are clearing thousands of years of outdated conditioning.* " —Paulina Serafina

RECEIVING PSYCHIC INFORMATION

Do you have a hard time controlling the amount of energy or intuitive guidance coming at you? As an empath develops and grows, they will become more and more energetically sensitive and will need to learn how to protect themselves from absorbing energy that they are picking up intuitively.

I learned this amazing little trick one day when I saw an umbrella opening and closing during meditation. I use it when I am ready to receive information that comes through during my private sessions and when I am ready to open myself up to guidance from the universe.

1. Close your eyes and picture a closed umbrella. Now, imagine it opening. This sends a visual signal that you are ready to receive information, impressions, or anything else that needs to come through your subtle bodies (see The Seven Bodies of Energy on page 106).

2. When you are ready to finish receiving information or guidance, visualize closing the umbrella and say a simple thank you.

The Shadow Self

According to astrologer Rebeca Eigen, the shadow self, "as defined by Carl G. Jung, is everything about us that is unconscious, unexpressed, denied, and repressed." All of us have a shadow self. When you are being moved through an awakening, you will be forced to take a good, long look at your shadow aspects—the not-so-fun parts of your personality that need to be worked on, the aspects of yourself that you really do not want to look at or may be too scared to face. However, by becoming conscious of your shadow self, you can truly understand yourself more, which leads to a more fulfilling life.

When you begin to accept and face your own shadow, this helps you to stop projecting your own wounding onto others so you can heal. Once you have faced your own fears, grown, and done the inner work that you need to do to get to the next level, you can begin to fully accept the shadow aspects of other individuals as well.

This is important, because when an empath begins to awaken to their natural gifts, they may have to face some things about themselves that they were not fully conscious of. Awakening is a purification process, so there may be some deep wounding that the empath did not realize they had to heal, such as projection issues, inner child wounding, and abandonment issues.

Take a moment to write down everything you may be scared of facing. Take a deep look at everything you wrote down, really have a look at it all. Know that you are giving yourself the opportunity to prove your worth, heal, and come back into alignment. By bringing your shadow attributes out into awareness, you now have the ability to face and heal them for good.

_____

_____

_____

_____

_____

Now take a moment to write down all of your gifts. Take a moment to be grateful for them and know that there is a purpose for them.

_____

_____

_____

_____

_____

_____

_____

Once you have finished writing out your shadow attributes and your gifts, on a separate piece of paper, write down everything you want to let go of. All of the fears, doubts, attachments, lower vibrational emotions and insecurities, and situations that are no longer serving you, etc. When you're done, burn the list.

While you are burning the list, you can say out loud to the universe: "Please take my fear and transmute it to love. I am now asking for your help to grow."

> **"** *In order to understand your divinity, you must first understand your humanity. We are a spectrum, and this is going to come out during an awakening.* **"** —Natalie Pachel

Spiritual Bypassing

When one goes through an awakening/ascension process, it can feel so overwhelming that a person can decide not to deal with issues that they are being called upon to heal head on. Focusing solely on the spiritual aspects of awakening and ignoring your own issues is something we call spiritual bypassing. According to psychologist John Welwood, spiritual bypassing is a "tendency to use spiritual ideas and practices to sidestep or avoid facing unresolved emotional issues, psychological wounds, and unfinished developmental tasks." This is something I have experienced on my own awakening journey, and I have witnessed numerous accounts of others experiencing this defense mechanism as well. It is a common occurrence.

Awakening is tough enough on its own. I totally understand. However, it is important not to hide away from that which has been illuminated and needs to be healed in your life.

None of us like to deal with pain, but it is the act of allowing ourselves to feel everything, even the pain, that helps us find clarity and figure out who we are. It helps us determine what serves us and what no longer serves us, so we can live in wholeness. This is what facing the shadow is all about. The sooner we get to work on facing and healing the shadow self, the sooner things will begin to turn in a positive direction.

Five Signs You May Be Spiritually Bypassing

1. You may be numbing yourself emotionally and not acknowledging the real pain you are feeling inside that needs to be sat with and looked at. This looks like pretending everything is okay when it simply is not.

2. You may have an obsession with fifth-dimensional talk and energy, failing to recognize that you are living in a three-dimensional world and need to focus on here-and-now, three-dimensional experiences. There is a reason you incarnated here into a physical world. It is necessary to stay grounded, in this moment and in your current reality. This is in no way saying that you cannot acknowledge the fifth dimension or a higher realm connection. I know how exciting it can be when you first start tapping into these energies, but you cannot hang out there all of the time. Balance is necessary.

3. You may overemphasize the positive side to enlightenment, claiming that nothing is negative. You do not want to talk about what needs to be discussed or looked at within your life so you can heal what needs to be healed.

4. You may be spiritually arrogant, thinking you are more enlightened than others are. Everyone is enlightened; we all just seem to notice at different times.

5. You may start detaching yourself from everything, not caring about anything and convincing yourself that everything will just work out. We are co-creators with the universe and we must take action toward the guidance that spirit offers to us. Without action, you can miss opportunities to align with that which you desire or that which is meant for you.

It is easy to become a spiritual bypasser because anything that ultimately helps us disconnect and keeps us from facing ourselves feels better.

It is important to acknowledge and recognize that spiritual bypassing is a real thing that many individuals experience. If any of the above signs resonate with you, it's okay. You are now aware that this may be something you are doing or have done. Now you can make the conscious decision to surrender to and learn from your experiences with it.

Once you have been moved through these lessons, another layer is peeled back, more healing occurs, and you can become more in tune with yourself.

Spiritual Alchemy

Alchemy is the process of turning worthless metals like lead into precious metals like gold. Similarly, spiritual alchemy is the transformation of consciousness. You can turn basic consciousness into a higher level of consciousness. Spiritual alchemy assists us with releasing basic egotistic needs, desires, and fears with love. This ultimately causes an individual to live from their heart and not their mind.

This is a process that those who awaken and many empaths are moved through because empaths are energetic alchemists. Empaths turn fear into love. Empaths turn that which is negative into positive, dark to light. Empaths: You are this powerful. You are not fragile; you are a warrior.

Empaths and Psychic Attack

If you are an empath, you will at some point experience psychic attack on your journey. A psychic attack is when an empath feels the negative energy coming from others; the energy is specifically being projected toward the empath. Most empaths do not know that this is what they are experiencing until much later on when they realize how sensitive and in tune they actually are.

There are a few ways that psychic attacks can occur, but one of the most common ways is through thought form exchanging.

Empaths are very susceptible to feeling when another is having undesirable thoughts about them or when low-vibrational, fear-based negative energy is being directed toward the empath. I have personally experienced this while awake and dreaming.

A psychic attack usually comes from people whom we know (whether they are conscious or unconscious of the energy they are sending), such as family members, friends, or acquaintances. It can also come from those that the empath no longer wants to associate with, and sometimes even those who do not know the empath personally but may have a mutual connection with someone that the empath does.

Most people do not pick up on the thoughts that others may be having about them, but because empaths are so sensitive to all types of energy, empaths pick up on this type of energy without even wanting or trying to.

One of the most common signs of a psychic attack is repetitive negative thoughts popping up in your mind several times a day about someone. This is usually an indicator that this person may be sending you negative energy or thinking bad thoughts about you or a situation that you may be involved in.

Another form of psychic attack is when someone is threatened by you standing in your power and would like to see you fail. These individuals may consciously spread negativity or low-vibrational energy with the intent to knock you down or dim your light.

Protecting Yourself from Psychic Attacks

If you sense you are experiencing a psychic attack, then try to put a stop to it as soon as possible. If not, you will feel exhausted, while the other person will most likely feel nothing at all. It is very important to note that psychic attacks will have little to no effect on you if you are standing in your full light and power, have a healthy self-esteem, and have a healthy aura.

Here are some tips for protecting against a psychic attack:

1. Do not direct negative thought patterns back at this individual. Instead, try to think of and do other things. Think of things that can shift your energetic pattern immediately. Remember, you ultimately have control over who and what you allow into your energy field.

2. Take a deep breath in, close your eyes, imagine all the energy that is being directed at you, and then blow it back toward the negative individual or situation.

3. Schedule yourself to receive a reiki treatment to see if there are any energetic cords that need to be cut. If there are, release them with love and light. (Learn more about cords and hooks on page 60.)

4. Each day, set a clear intention to attract only people or situations that are for your highest good.

5. Do whatever you can to keep your energetic field (your aura) strong. Your energy field is affected by how you feel, so it is important to keep your emotions based in love as much as possible. Leading a healthy lifestyle that serves you and allows you to keep yourself feeling good and positive will help keep your energetic field healthy. Keep your energetic field strong by:

- Eating healthy, high vibrational foods such as fresh fruits and vegetables
- Practicing daily exercise to help combat lower-density energy
- Controlling your environment as much as possible; make sure you are around only those who are uplifting and help you feel energized
- Staying away from drugs or alcohol
- Practicing gratitude; think about what you are grateful for in this moment, and focus on what you are looking forward to
- Practicing self-love and care

Daily Routines to Protect Your Energy

Wake-up cording routine. As soon as you start your day, sit up out of bed and establish a new grounding cord. Visualize a beautiful white and gold light coming down through your crown chakra and out through the bottom of your feet. Imagine the cord growing and expanding down into the earth. I like to imagine it going through crystal caves and then plugging into the earth's core.

Now you have a cord that is with you all day. So if you encounter negative energy or a negative situation during the day, you have a place to "flush" it. Take a moment to inhale some light and imagine all of the negative energy being flushed down out of your body and into the center of the earth for transmutation.

Shower meditation. Water is incredibly refreshing and cleansing. Set an intention for your shower time. What do you want to cleanse? Imagine the shower being white light and it washing away the negative or lower vibrational energy off of you and down the drain. Literally visualize anything negative—thoughts, emotions, situations—falling away from you.

Energy bubble. I like to create an energetic bubble for myself that expands outward from my heart chakra. Imagine the light from inside your heart chakra expanding and creating an egg- or bubble-shaped shield that reaches a few inches outside of your body. If you have to do this a few times a day, do it. I'll visualize this bubble protecting me again and again when I am around someone who may not be in the best space energetically so I can avoid absorbing what they are carrying.

Salt or crystal baths. Soak with Epsom salt and your crystals a few times a week. Epsom salt is grounding and the crystals you choose will help bring you back into a place of balance as well. A lot of my clients like to soak with big pieces of rose quartz. When you empty the bath, imagine all of the energy that does not serve you leaving you and washing down the drain.

Daily or nightly cord cutting. If you have created a grounding cord for yourself and have been visualizing negative energy being flushed down it throughout the day, it may be a good idea at some point to call upon Archangel Michael (see page 114) to cut it away from you and then repeat the process of anchoring back in- creating a new cord. A lot of my clients like to do this at the end of a long day.

Energetic boundaries. If you find yourself around a person who may be draining or projecting, excuse yourself as soon as you can, or be direct with the person who may be affecting you. Explain to them that you cannot be around this type of energy. I had a beautiful soul once tell me that when he comes across others who are too heightened for him, he uses this phrase: "I choose not to experience what you are experiencing right now." Then, he either leaves the situation or hangs up the phone. I find that phrase to be direct and totally perfect. It will certainly cause the other person to think about what they are doing while you are establishing a healthy boundary for yourself.

Take time to be alone. Everyone needs alone time, but this is crucial for an empath. Do not allow others to take all of your time away. Make it your intention to go for a daily walk, do a daily meditation, enjoy daily bath time, or do whatever resonates best with you. It is not selfish, it is necessary.

CHAPTER EIGHT

Empaths, Energy, and Spirituality

As you learned earlier in the book, everything is energy. But there are many types of energy for an empath to be aware of, and many ways that empaths can tap into these energies. And as empaths connect more to the energies around them, they become more connected to the divine.

The Seven Bodies of Energy

It is important for an empath to know about the subtle bodies of energy around them. When an empath is aware of how to balance and harness their own energy and energy fields, they will be less likely to experience burnout. There are seven bodies of energy: physical, etheric, emotional astral, mental, casual, spiritual, and divine light.

1. Physical body

The physical body is most dense. It is the vessel where the soul is held while incarnated. Taking care of the physical body is essential. Those who are awakening often focus mainly on tuning into the higher dimensional bodies and neglect the physical body, but it is also important to maintain the physical body, be sure to eat well, exercise, and drink plenty of water.

2. Etheric body

The etheric body, or emotional body, is a double of the physical body. Think of it like a battery for the physical body. It is crucial to keep this body clean and clear, because the etheric body can become congested with negative thinking. When this happens, you can become more susceptible to disease, uncertainty, fatigue, and worry. To maintain the etheric body, make sure you watch your thought patterns. Make sure you are thinking positively or using affirmations as often as possible. It's also important to stay away from drugs. Drugs can actually cause the etheric body to become weaker, which can make an individual be more susceptible to lower vibrational energy. Also, maintain a healthy diet with a proper intake of vitamins and supplements.

3. Emotional astral body

The emotional astral body relates to feelings, desires, and emotions. You can run into conflict here when you place the desires of the ego over the desires of the heart. To maintain the emotional astral body, be sure to honor your heart, engage in daily meditation, and stay grounded and balanced emotionally.

4. Mental body

The mental body relates to your mind. It is important to keep the mind as calm as possible so you can discern what is truth and what is illusion. For a strong mental body, keep your thoughts focused only on that which you want to manifest.

Only take in or allow positive thoughts to dwell. If it feels good, let it in. If it doesn't, let it go. Surround yourself with positive people or situations; do not allow negativity to work its way in and stay there with you.

5. Casual body

The casual body is the "soul temple," so to speak. This body holds the collection of experiences your soul has had. This is where your karma is stored. Higher knowledge is here and it vibrates higher than the other bodies. To maintain the casual body, be sure to listen to and honor your intuition. Drop the needs and wants of the lower self so your higher self and soul truth can manifest. Claim what is meant for you so you can align with your soul growth rewards. Meditate so information that has been lying dormant within you can be awakened and accessed.

6. Spiritual body

The spiritual body represents divine love and spiritual ecstasy. As we begin to raise our level of awareness and step into new levels of consciousness, we begin to access this body. To maintain the spiritual body, always live from the heart, show unconditional love for yourself and others, and work to understand and accept the interconnectedness of all things.

7. Divine light body

The divine light body vibrates at a very high speed. When you are in touch with this body, you understand that we are all one with the divine. This body is the body that contains Kundalini energy—the life force energy that runs up and down the spine. To maintain the divine light body, try to go with the flow of life and relinquish the illusion of control. Drink plenty of water, eat high vibrational whole foods, and take Epsom salt baths to stay clear and stay in your heart center.

What Is Kundalini Energy?

Kundalini is a life force energy. Also known as prana or chi, Kundalini is a Sanskrit word that identifies the rising of an energy that is coiled at the base of the spine. It is believed that we carry this energy with us from the time we are born until it is released at the time of passing.

Remember, we are electrical beings. Imagine your chakras as running on an electrical board or circuit system of some kind. As Kundalini energy rises and travels up your spine, the energy passes through each chakra, giving them an energy boost and causing them to ignite, or light up.

When this type of energy rise happens, deep healing begins to take place on all levels. (Learn more about chakras in Chapter 9.)

When Kundalini energy awakens, you are taken through a series of shifts. Deep emotional healing occurs, causing you to heal and align more with the vibration of love. When this happens, intuition and psychic gifts can begin to develop or expand because you are vibrating farther and farther away from fear-based emotions. If you were born with psychic gifts and they have been suppressed due to traumas you have not healed from yet, get ready for your gifts to come through tenfold, and prepare yourself for quite the eye-opening experience. Your intuition will be coming through and your mind can have a very hard time understanding this. Go with the flow and look at the experience as an adventure. You are being moved through all of it for a reason.

Various types of deep healing can occur. For example, you will have the chance to fully heal from past traumas and deeply held wounds, such as feelings of abandonment, insecurities, or false beliefs about yourself. That's right, this means that the devastating and heartbreaking event that you swore you were "over" years ago will come up again for healing and transmutation. You will literally feel everything all over again until you have cleansed yourself of the lower vibrational energy associated with it.

You may be called upon to love yourself more and be asked to take a look at what is serving your heart and what is not. Boundaries, codependent behaviors, triggers, and self-worth issues will be called upon for you to work on. You may be called to forgive yourself and others. It can actually begin to feel like a necessity. You will be called upon to listen to and follow your heart, become more in touch with your intuition, and heal your attachment issues, emotional or physical. As you feel your psychic senses awakening, you will begin to embody unconditional love, not just for yourself, but for everyone. Logic will begin to play less of a role in your life. You will begin to feel more and think less.

As Kundalini energy moves through you, it affects your seven main chakras. These are some indicators of which chakras are being healed:

Root Chakra: You will start facing fears about being unstable and insecurities about providing for yourself.

Sacral Chakra: You will start birthing something new, feeling creativity, and honoring the feminine energy of creation.

Solar Plexus: You will start becoming a stronger and more capable version of yourself, feeling greater self-confidence and willpower.

Heart Chakra: You will learn how to love yourself more, honor your heart, and begin inner child healing.

Throat Chakra: You will learn how to speak your truth, stand in your authenticity, and be true to your soul.

Third Eye Chakra: You will feel your psychic gifts growing and expanding. Clairvoyant gifts may open up. You will start seeing things during meditation or colors and sparks around others.

Crown Chakra: You will start receiving downloads and divinely inspired ideas, which comes with a realization that you are one with the divine. You will feel clarity coming through; you will see things more clearly, from a higher perspective.

Kundalini energy is known for its transformative power. When one is moved through a Kundalini awakening, it is a transformational soul experience. A person is usually never the same again. They usually experience some kind of rebirth, because the amount of healing they have been moved through on a soul level causes their vibration to rise. It's important to note that not everyone experiences a Kundalini awakening, but in my experience, many empaths and sensitive souls experience this return to divine source energy.

Does this sound like something you are experiencing?

　　　　　○ YES　　　　○ NO

Write a brief description about your personal experiences:

_____

_____

_____

_____

_____

_____

_____

_____

> " *When we meditate, we are raising the Kundalini through focus, through concentration. There is a metaphysical astral process that is taking place.* "
> —Frederick Lenz

Empaths and Light Work

If you are an empath, odds are you are some type of a light worker. This is not always the case, but the empaths I have worked with tend to feel a strong desire to serve and share their light and gifts in some way.

A light worker is a soul that has been moved through an awakening at some point on their journey. They are conscious and want to devote their life to serving others in a way that fills and nourishes their own soul as well. Light workers carry the flame of light within them and use this light to help enlighten others.

A light worker makes the decision to follow the call of their heart, moving toward love light; they do not allow the mind to control them and draw them toward fear and darkness.

It's important to note that light workers come in all types of different shapes and sizes. I have met many light workers who are not practicing intuitives, but instead decide to share their light through creative endeavors such as music and art, teaching others, or by simply spreading positive energy everywhere they go.

QUIZ: ARE YOU A LIGHT WORKER?

1. Do you feel that you are here to help guide or heal others?	○ YES	○ NO
2. Do you feel that you are here for a higher purpose or that there is something you are meant to accomplish?	○ YES	○ NO
3. Have you learned what it means to walk by faith and not so much by sight? You have literally been moved through the lesson of learning to believe in miracles.	○ YES	○ NO

4. Did you have an intense childhood full of many traumas or other difficulties? Often, light workers come into an understanding that the difficulties that they experienced were not intended to hurt them, but rather served to awaken and help them to become the light worker they are today.

◯ YES   ◯ NO

5. Do you feel like you are on a constant mission to improve your life, the lives of those you love, and the lives of others?

◯ YES   ◯ NO

6. Do you love giving to others in any way you can? A lot of light workers love giving to friends, family, and total strangers.

◯ YES   ◯ NO

7. Do you feel a strong connection to animals? You may even find yourself attracting stray animals, petting wild animals, or helping animals in some way.

◯ YES   ◯ NO

8. Do you feel a strong connection to nature? Light workers will often find themselves sad or terribly upset when they see trees being cut down or nature being destroyed by man.

◯ YES   ◯ NO

9. At some point in your life, have you experienced an intense spiritual awakening that forced you to purge all of your self-limiting beliefs and perceived weaknesses? Did you shed anything that was holding you back from living in alignment with love?

◯ YES   ◯ NO

10. Have you ever envisioned wrapping someone you love or even a total stranger in white light as you walked or drove by them?

◯ YES   ◯ NO

> When I was a little girl if I saw someone on the side of the road and it looked like they needed help, I would imagine sending them white light from my heart and wrapping it around them.

If you answered yes to 5 out of these 10 questions, you're most likely a light worker.

Briefly describe your feelings about this. What do you think your purpose is as a light worker?

_____

_____

_____

_____

A Light Worker's Creed

I am a Light worker

I awoke so that others may awaken

I learn so that others may also learn

I transform so others may transform

I lighten my load so that others may change theirs

I learn to see so that others may also see

I forgave myself so that I may help others to forgive

I love myself so I can bring out love in others

I AM a Light worker

I live to give comfort

I live to shine loving light onto others

I live to heal

I live to give hope

I live for truth

I live for love

—Unknown

---

66 *Because of love, I became the giver of light.* **99** —Rumi

The Empath's Angel

There are many archangels available to call upon when you are growing and developing on your journey, but if you are an empath, especially one who is spiritually inclined, it is good to know about Archangel Muriel.

Archangel Muriel's name means perfume of God. Muriel is a very powerful yet gentle angel who is connected to highly sensitive and empathic souls who are ready to open up and advance their intuitive gifts to the next level. When Muriel is around you may notice your clairalience (gift of clear smelling) coming through. I first noticed Muriel during meditation, but since then, I will notice subtle smells of flowers every now and again when Muriel is around.

Archangel Muriel will work with an empath to develop their gift of clairsentience. Muriel teaches you and guides you to trust in the infinite wisdom of your own heart. Muriel helps empaths develop clarity and brings about an increased passion to act in the direction of their life purpose.

In addition to our own guardian angel, empaths can seek out the beautiful blessings of other archangels. As you develop your spiritual gifts and feel more connected to divine energy, you may want to call upon some of these other archangels.

It is important to remember that the angels are always waiting for you to call upon them. They will not interfere with your free will unless you ask for help. So if you desire assistance, make sure you take the time to ask for their help, daily if needed. Here are other archangels you can call upon:

Archangel Michael. Archangel Michael is one of the most well-known archangels. He helps protect us and shield us from that which is not serving us. Call upon Archangel

Michael to help shield you and cut the cords to anything that is no longer serving you in life. Michael can also be called upon to assist you with setting clear intentions for yourself.

Archangel Raphael. Archangel Raphael is an archangel that I call upon a lot for healing. Raphael helps us heal our hearts and works very closely with healers. Call upon Archangel Raphael when you or a loved one are in need of healing, whether physically or emotionally.

Archangel Metatron. Archangel Metatron is the teacher of esoteric knowledge and uses sacred geometry to assist those who are sensitive. If you are trying to grasp higher levels of learning, Metatron is excellent to call upon. Metatron uses the Merkabah cube for healing.

Archangel Chamuel. Archangel Chamuel is the angel of peace. Chamuel reminds us that peace comes from within and helps us remember that love is the only thing that is real. Chamuel can help you with your life purpose and help you attain what you ask for, as long as it is in alignment with your higher path. Call upon Chamuel when trying to get into alignment with what you would like to manifest into the physical from the heart.

Archangel Ariel. Archangel Ariel is the angel of healing, prosperity, and destiny. I often see Ariel during meditation when I am being guided to follow my intuition regarding creative endeavors so I can manifest what I need into the physical. Call upon Ariel to help give you the strength you need to follow your intuition.

Archangel Gabriel. Archangel Gabriel assists with motivation. Gabriel works closely with teachers, writers, messengers, artists, and those who counsel and serve others. Gabriel works closely with divine feminine energy. Call upon Gabriel when you need a loving push to polish up on your skills.

Archangel Uriel. Archangel Uriel is the angel of ideas. Uriel often guides us with inspired ideas or epiphanies. Call upon Uriel when you are in need of a divinely inspired idea. Uriel is associated with the gift of claircognizance.

Archangel Jophiel. Archangel Jophiel is the angel of all things beautiful. Jophiel assists with feelings of gratitude. Call upon Jophiel when you need help incorporating more positivity and appreciation into your life. Jophiel will also help you see the beauty within yourself.

Archangel Sandalphon. Archangel Sandalphon helps you develop your spirituality and get closer to your loving creator. Sandalphon helps you feel divine love and feel secure. Sandalphon works with us to listen to our hearts.

Archangel Azrael. Archangel Azrael assists during times of grief and transition. Call upon Azrael during times of loss/transition, when heart healing is needed. If anything is blocking your spiritual growth, Azrael will help you distinguish between truth and illusions.

Archangel Raziel. Archangel Raziel is an angel who can help you reclaim your power. Raziel assists in healing past pains and hurts, especially if they create fear of moving toward your life purpose. Call upon Raziel when you are in healing mode and are ready to step into personal empowerment.

Archangel Zadkiel. Archangel Zadkiel is a powerful healer of the mind and is associated with the gift of clairaudience. Zadkiel will give you gentle and loving guidance toward your mission. Zadkiel helps you shift from a victim mindset to one of forgiveness and empowerment. Call upon Zadkiel when you are ready to take responsibility for yourself.

Archangel Haniel. Archangel Haniel, associated with the gift of clairvoyance, assists with developing your intuition. Haniel aids with sacred feminine energy and learning to trust your inner guidance.

Archangel Jeremiel. Archangel Jeremiel assists you with seeing the divine light within yourself and others. Call upon Jeremiel when you need to take inventory of your life and review what you need to do to make positive future plans. Jeremiel will help you with transition and change. If you find yourself stuck at all on your spiritual path, Jeremiel will help with a renewed sense of passion and motivation.

Archangel Raguel. Archangel Raguel helps you see past illusions. Raguel can help you heal relationships with others as well as the relationship you hold with yourself. Call upon Raguel when you need help bringing harmony into your life.

> 66 *God and the archangels know your heart, they know what is in your heart before you even speak it. You don't have to say a word, or say the right words, they already know everything you have been through and everything your heart truly wants to experience.* 99 —Eileen Anglin

CHAPTER NINE

Meditation and Chakra Healing for Empaths

It is important for everyone to know about chakras, or the energy vortexes that we all have, especially if you are an empath. Chakras will help an empath understand how to manage their own energetic field. In this chapter, you will learn about each chakra and the function it holds, how to tell when it is in or out of balance, and what you can do to maintain optimum flow for yourself.

I recommend working on developing one chakra every day, and one of the best ways to do that is through meditation. You can start with the root and work your way up to the crown, or work in whichever order you'd like. The important part is that you do some sort of meditation practice daily.

When I first awakened to a deeper understanding of what I am and what role I was to play here, I was intuitively guided to start meditating. Like so many, I had a very hard time shutting down my mind (although I later discovered that "shutting down the mind" is the very opposite of what should be done during meditation; meditation is about allowing yourself to observe everything that comes up in your mind), so I was guided to listen to binaural beats at night to open myself up to the experience. Within a few months, meditation became a daily practice. I started with a simple seven-minute divine love heart-opening meditation, which you can find on YouTube, then moved on to daily guided chakra meditations.

What are the benefits of meditation for empaths? To put it simply, meditation is a great way for you to learn about energy, tune into your own heart space (which is essential for discernment), awaken your intuitive gifts, and gain clarity for creating something new in your life. Let's take a deeper look at meditation before discussing the individual chakras.

What Is Meditation?

Think of meditation as a way to reboot your mind. Meditation is allowing yourself to get into a calm state, focus on your own breath, and tune into your own vibration. There are so many ways to meditate. There is the traditional way that many of us know: sitting down, closing your eyes, and opening up to whatever comes through. However, a meditative state can also be achieved by going out for a walk or hike, connecting with nature, or doing yoga or any other activity that allows you to connect to your source of energy.

There is no single, right way to meditate. But it's important to note that if you go into meditation with the intention of "clearing your mind" and "not thinking," it will not work. The key to meditation is to allow whatever thoughts come up to flow through you. Often, this is how intuitive psychic empaths will begin to understand their signs and symbols

for reading energy, so take note of all you see, no matter how illogical it may seem; you are seeing what you see for a reason. Write down what you are seeing in a journal, and then when you are done with your meditation session, spend the time looking up the meanings of all you saw.

For example, if you see a shape, symbol, or animal totem, look up the spiritual meaning of that item and there will be a message there for you. Before I could begin to help others, I had to learn what my signs and symbols were so I could process a reading or healing effectively and efficiently. If you are meant to share your psychic gifts and continue your path as a healer, you may eventually see these symbols or signs while in a non-meditative state, as well. If you are not on that path, this type of meditation exercise is still an amazing way to receive messages and guidance while on your own personal journey.

EXERCISE: MEDITATION FOR BEGINNERS

1. Sit down or lie comfortably so your spine is aligned and straight. If sitting up, place your hands on each knee, palms up. I recommend sitting on a cushion. If lying down, keep your hands close to your sides.

2. Close your eyes and begin to focus on your breath. Do not manipulate your breathing, just focus on your breath at its natural pace. Observe your chest, shoulders, rib cage, and belly. Feel your breath going in and out of you. It is fine if you would like to imagine yourself somewhere that you love, but it is not necessary. Just keep focusing on your breath.

3. Begin to notice any thoughts or images that are arising. This is normal. Allow the thoughts to come and go. Just observe them. If you begin to feel as though you are overthinking, just take a deep breath and come back to focusing on the breath going in and out of the center of your chest. Keep observing what arises.

Tip: When I have a negative thought come up during meditation, I imagine wrapping it in white light and then throwing it out.

4. Keep a journal next to you. Write down anything you see, hear, or experience as you meditate.

Time: Aim to meditate for five to seven minutes in the beginning, with the goal of working up to 25 to 30 minutes of daily meditation if possible.

What did you see or experience while meditating? Did you see colors or shapes? Animals or insects? Symbols, names, faces, characters, or words? What did you feel? What did you hear? It's important to know that you can see anything while meditating and everyone is different.

_____

_____

_____

_____

_____

How are you feeling after your meditation?

_____

_____

_____

_____

_____

66*Prayer is when you talk to God, meditation is when God talks to you.*99
—Unknown

Breath of Fire Technique

Breath of Fire (Pranayama) is one of the foundational breath techniques that is used in the practice of Kundalini yoga. This technique is all about continuous, rapid, rhythmic breathing. It is an ancient technique that is used frequently in modern day practices as a cleansing ritual. I like to imagine everything that I want to rid myself of, any doubt, worry, or anxiety, literally melting off of my body when I do this technique. I feel fantastic afterward and full of energy.

Breath of fire helps to strengthen the solar plexus, release toxins, relieve chronic pain, repair the balance between the sympathetic and parasympathetic nervous systems, increase oxygen flow to the brain, significantly reduce stress, increase physical activity, and reduce addictive impulses.

HOW TO DO BREATH OF FIRE

1. Sit up tall. Lengthen the space between your belly button and your heart chakra.

2. Breathe in and out through your nose. Inhale for the same amount of time that you exhale. For example, if you breathe in for three seconds, breathe out for three seconds. Pull your abs in during the exhale and then press your abs out during the inhale. Visualize your stomach filling up with air during the inhale and then using your ab muscles to push the air out during the exhale. It takes a moment to get used to this, but you will get it!

3. Once you have gotten into a rhythm, start to shorten your breaths and pick up the pace. Your breathing should be loud and quick. Make sure your inhalations and exhalations are balanced in both strength and length.

4. After a while of practicing the breath of fire breathing technique, you can move up toward doing two or three sets of the Breath of Fire, with a few long breaths in between.

It is normal to feel tingling during Breath of Fire. Some may experience feeling a little light headed. If so, take a few deep breaths and try to relax. Once the exercise is completed, you should feel like your mind is very clear.

It is important to note that it takes time to build up to full Breath of Fire. It took me two or three weeks to really get the hang of it, so give yourself time. Beginners should start with a shorter amount of time and at a slower rate.

It is also important to know that it is recommended to avoid Breath of Fire if you are pregnant, struggle with vertigo, or have a high blood pressure.

What Are Chakras?

Chakras are points within our physical bodies where energy flows through us. It is important to keep these energy points healthy and flowing openly. In Sanskrit, the word chakra literally means "spinning wheel or disk." If any one of your chakras experiences a blockage, you will most likely experience emotional or physical symptoms, which can keep you from living in alignment with what is meant for you. For example, you may not be able to follow your heart or speak your truth. The result of these two blockages—a blocked heart chakra (difficulty loving the self and others) and the inability to get into alignment with your mission—can lead to depression and thyroid disorders.

A study published in the *Journal of Consciousness Exploration & Research*, headed by Dr. Pradeep B. Deshpande, involving over 100 participants, measured the amount of energy coming out of each chakra. Researchers used a software called Biowell to decipher whether the participants had healthy auras or leaks in their chakras. This study shows that the energetic field can be measured. Keeping your energetic body and chakras healthy leads to a stronger empath—one who is less susceptible to absorbing other people's energy, better able to maintain balance, and can be more empowered.

Each chakra is connected to the central nervous system and conducts energy, known as Kundalini energy, or serpent power. The function of the eight main chakras is very intricate. They are an energy system that communicates with the body using biological systems such as the endocrine glands and the nervous system. The endocrine system is a network of glands that is in charge of producing, regulating, and distributing hormones throughout our body. Each of the chakras in the body is paired with a gland and helps to govern its overall function.

In the following pages, I will talk about the seven main chakras—the root chakra, sacral chakra, solar plexus chakra, heart chakra, throat chakra, third eye chakra, and crown chakra—as well as the foot chakra.

Root Chakra

The root chakra is associated with the earth, stability, and survival. It is where we gain our sense of security from. If you are trusting, independent, and find yourself to be grounded, you can rest assured that you most likely have balanced root chakra energy. However, if you are consistently in a state of fear, frustration, or worry, this is an indicator that your root chakra energy is out of balance and you are not grounded. This tends to be an area in need of development for many of the empaths I have worked with, myself included.

The root chakra is connected with the adrenal glands, which are responsible for our fight-or-flight response; this instinctive response to a threatening situation either tells you to resist with force or run away. The adrenal glands are made up of two parts. The outer part is called the adrenal cortex and the inner part is called the adrenal medulla. The adrenal cortex produces hormones, such as cortisol, that regulate the body's metabolism. The adrenal medulla produces hormones that help the body deal with physical and emotional stress by increasing the body's heart rate and blood pressure.

Healthy and balanced adrenal glands help us stay grounded and calm, and support our parasympathetic nervous system. Similarly, a healthy and balanced root chakra keeps you grounded and calm.

Balancing the Root Chakra

In addition to meditating with a focus on the root chakra, there are several other activities you can incorporate into your daily routine to help keep you grounded.

1. Grounding. Walk around barefoot on the ground and connect yourself to the earth. You are an energetic being. You need to be grounded so all that energy you have within you doesn't cause a burnout, which in turn causes fear and anxiety. Walking or standing on the earth for at least five minutes a day will help you feel calmer, more stable, and less like you are "out of your body" so you can focus and accomplish what you need to for the day. You can also use a grounding pad.

These wonderful little inventions are meant for you to sleep on. They provide all of the benefits of grounding and can help with your sleep patterns, which is something that many empaths battle with due to having a hard time unwinding after a stimulating day.

2. Bring yourself back to this very moment. When we live in anything but the moment, it causes us depression or anxiety. One of my favorite exercises to do when I am feeling fearful is to close my eyes, inhale white light, and then imagine blowing it out of my heart chakra, creating a shield around me. It allows me to get back into touch with my body. When I am focused on feeling my body in that very moment, no other thoughts are distracting me.

3. Do something physical. Get outside, go for a run, practice some yoga—whatever you do, it is important to get moving! Physical exercise helps because it gives your energy somewhere to go. Also, when you do physical activity, you are focused on what you are doing in that very moment instead of sitting around in thinking mode. You are feeling, which often brings a lot of clarity and "aha" type of moments because you are more connected.

4. Release notes. Take some time to journal or write out what you would like to release. Once you have written down what you would like to release, take the paper outside and burn it in a safe place. This not only sends that energy out to be transmuted, but it also creates a physical anchored memory within you: You have chosen to consciously release what needed to be released. This is beneficial, because if you should find yourself falling back into that same worry or fear, you can quickly remind yourself that you already released that and you will remember that you have a choice to repeat the cycle or not.

Root Chakra Affirmations

- ❖ I am calm, I am stable, I am grounded
- ❖ I have all that I need
- ❖ I am open to new possibilities and opportunities
- ❖ I trust
- ❖ I am deeply rooted
- ❖ I belong here

- ❖ I have purpose
- ❖ I am right where I am supposed to be in this moment
- ❖ I am powerful
- ❖ I am safe
- ❖ I am worthy and capable of achieving abundance on all levels

Sacral Chakra

This vortex is associated with water, passion, movement, and creation. If you go with the flow of life and are sexually fulfilled, naturally playful, and trust the process of life, you can rest assured, you most likely have balanced sacral chakra energy. However, if you have a need to control, are overly concerned with what others think of you, or do not feel fulfilled on a passionate level, this is an indicator that your sacral chakra is out of balance.

The sacral chakra is associated with the gonads: the ovaries in a female and the testicles in a male. This is our main source of sexual hormones, causing new life to be created.

For women, it is important to note that there is a direct connection between the ovaries and the adrenal glands. A woman's menstrual cycle can be heavily affected by adrenal fatigue (page 82).

According to Christiane Northrup, M.D., our thoughts and feelings are linked to our physical body through our endocrine system. If we are ignoring or suppressing our intuition, we can have problems within the sacral chakra area; for example, we may experience ovarian cysts that are caused by energetic blockages.

I have personally had some serious issues with my sacral chakra energy until I finally started to listen to and trust in my intuition and allow things to flow in my life, without needing to control things or rely on external validation from others. I have also worked with many other empaths with this same issue.

Balancing the Sacral Chakra

In addition to meditating with a focus on the sacral chakra, there are several other activities you can incorporate into your daily routine to help with creative flow and passion.

1. Step into your creative power. This chakra is all about honoring creation. It doesn't matter what you are creating, just create. You do not have to be an artist in order to create. If I am feeling stagnant at all, I will make jewelry, sing, write, or spend some time in meditation visualizing what I would like to create so I can align with and manifest it.

2. Honor and embrace your sexuality. We are human, we have desires, and we are meant to align with passion and fulfillment. Do not suppress this aspect of yourself—there is

real healing that occurs when it comes to honoring what we truly desire. Trust in what or who you feel passionate about in your love life, as long as the connection is a healthy one that is of equal energy exchange.

3. Go with the flow of life. This chakra is associated with creation and the power of the sacred feminine energy. The feminine knows the power of flowing; she does not force or attempt to control life. She honors her intuition and she invites creation.

4. Do sacral chakra stretching or Kundalini yoga. The Breath of Fire technique is a Kundalini yoga practice; see page 120. Butterfly stretching is excellent for sacral chakra healing.

5. Allow yourself to feel. Do not suppress your emotions. Your emotions are a map that you are born with, a guide to indicate what serves you and what doesn't. Honor your blueprint.

Sacral Chakra Affirmations

❖ I honor what I am feeling

❖ I embrace what and who I feel passionate about

❖ I give myself permission to feel pleasure

❖ I am abundant

❖ I am a sacred and sexual being

❖ I love my body

❖ I understand that my emotions are my body's way of communicating direction to me

❖ I am enough

❖ I am worthy of healthy and satisfying relationships

❖ I honor my creativity

Solar Plexus Chakra

This vortex is associated with fire, self-confidence, and a strong will. If you have a strong sense of self respect, willpower, and confidence about what to do in life, you can rest assured, you most likely have balanced solar plexus chakra energy. However, if you have low self-esteem, procrastinate, or find yourself being taken advantage of, your solar plexus chakra may be out of balance.

The solar plexus chakra is connected with the adrenal glands and the pancreas gland. As discussed on page 82, healthy and balanced adrenal glands help us stay grounded and calm, and support our parasympathetic nervous system. The pancreas, which helps with digestion and hormone production, is located slightly below and behind the stomach. The exocrine pancreas releases digestive enzymes, while the endocrine pancreas releases hormones that regulate the sugar levels in the blood. Diabetes is a common side effect of a poorly functioning pancreas.

Balancing the Solar Plexus Chakra

In addition to meditating with a focus on the solar plexus, there are several other activities you can incorporate into your daily routine to help boost self-confidence and willpower.

1. Breath of Fire. I love this exercise. This is a powerful tool. Breath of Fire helps us with breathing out the blocks that are held within. See page 120 to learn how to do Breath of Fire.

2. Exercise. It is absolutely essential for everyone to get daily exercise but if you are an empath, this is something you really cannot take a break from. Daily movement helps with adrenal fatigue, which is something many empaths suffer from (in fact, I have yet to meet an empath that doesn't suffer from this). Exercise is essential to get an increase in energy, serotonin, and dopamine levels. I enjoy running and cardio workouts, but whatever feels right for you, do that. Just get yourself moving every day. Dance and yoga are wonderful tools, as well.

3. Daily affirmations. When you are working on building up your self-confidence and willpower, it is important to have your mind in a healthy place. Incorporating a simple technique like looking at yourself in the mirror daily and repeating affirmations can be quite powerful. I also encourage hanging positive affirmations or positive quotes in your daily living space to remind you about what you are working on. I've recommended specific affirmations for the solar plexus chakra, but you can use any of the affirmations suggested throughout this book, or create your own! Whatever works for you is best.

4. Music, music, and more music. When I have a goal I am trying to reach, and when I need to stand in my full power, I listen to the most upbeat and positive music that I can. I match my music choices to my end goal. So when I am in empowerment mode, I choose music that is about empowerment. When I am writing about the vibration of love, it's music about love. I absorb those vibrations, I shift instantly, and my goal is attained with more flow.

5. Cutting cords. We are often emotionally tied to situations in our lives that can keep us caught in a negative cycle, feeling as if we cannot achieve something or that we are not good enough. There may also even be anchored memories from when we were young that keep us from trusting ourselves to achieve something on our own. Doing a cord cutting ceremony, keeping yourself away from these negative people and situations from the past, and consciously acknowledging our experiences but deciding that they are no longer going to affect us can be incredibly powerful when working on the solar plexus.

Solar Plexus Chakra Affirmations

❖ I am in control of my life, I am balanced

❖ I stand up for myself

❖ I choose happiness

❖ I love and accept myself

❖ I own my power

❖ I appreciate my gifts, talents, and strengths

❖ I am worthy of love

❖ I make my own choices

❖ I am not a victim

❖ I am free to choose in any situation I find myself in

Heart Chakra

This vortex is associated with air and unconditional love, and is referred to as the center. If you have a strong sense of self-worth and you choose love over fear, you can rest assured, you most likely have balanced heart chakra energy. However, if you feel unloved, indulge in self-pity, are needy or clingy, or you find yourself giving too much for validation (especially if you are engaged in an unhealthy codependent relationship), your heart chakra may be out of balance.

The heart chakra is connected with the thymus gland, which is considered to be the master gland when it comes to having a healthy immune system. The thymus gland produces white blood cells called T cells that fight infections and have the ability to destroy abnormal cells in the body. Science has proven that the T cell count increases when we are experiencing the positive emotions of giving and receiving love.

The thymus is considered to be "the seat of the soul," and it is powerfully affected by feeling and emotions. When we are feeling low-vibrational emotions such as anger and hate, our ability to fight off infection, inflammation, and disease is reduced and we become worn down. However, if we have forgiven both ourselves and others and focus on living in the center, our ability to fight off disease and inflammation rises.

Balancing the Heart Chakra

In addition to meditating with a focus on the heart chakra, there are several other activities you can incorporate into your daily routine to help develop your unconditional love and self-acceptance.

1. Honor your heart. Always honor what your heart is saying to you. You feel the way you feel for a reason. Your heart is a direct connection to the source and will lead you by giving you intuitive nudges in the direction your soul wants to go. Sometimes this can involve pain, but it is necessary so we can truly figure out who we are. Those who can live from their heart have the ability to create the life they've always wanted and deserve. It's about training the mind to become a servant to the heart.

2. Acknowledge your self-worth. You are worthy of abundance on every level. You deserve an equal exchange of energy in every aspect of your life, including relationships. Accept balance and do not give more than you get from any connection in your life. Believe in yourself and know that you are deserving of love.

3. Do things that make you feel good. When you feel like you are starting to get down or stress is taking over, simply shift the energy by doing something that makes you feel good. Exercising, enjoying music, going out with friends, or simply allowing yourself to be silly can help you shift in an instant. When you feel good, you shift into a frequency of abundance, which naturally attracts more abundance to come into your life.

4. Allow yourself to receive. More often than not, we pray and ask the universe for what we want but wind up blocking it from coming in due to our attachments, expectations on how it will arrive, or fears of not getting what we want. For example, you may desire more money or some other type of abundance to come into your life, but you still refuse to listen to your intuition or take steps toward a career or lifestyle change. Or, you may be always giving to others but never allowing yourself to receive.

Set clear intentions by listening to your heart. Allow what comes into your life to come and allow what goes out of your life to go; it is all for a reason.

5. Trust. Trust in your own wisdom and value. Trust in the gifts and insight you've been given—they have been given to you for a reason. You are an infinite being and the insights you have are for a purpose.

Heart Chakra Affirmations

- ❖ I accept things the way they are in this very moment
- ❖ I love myself unconditionally
- ❖ I nurture and honor my inner child
- ❖ I forgive myself and the others who have hurt me
- ❖ I allow love to guide all of my intentions and actions

- ❖ I am wanted and loved
- ❖ I walk my path centered and open
- ❖ I have healthy boundaries
- ❖ I am grateful for all of the challenges that helped me grow, transform, and open up to love
- ❖ I am love

Throat Chakra

This vortex is associated with communication and self-expression. If you have the ability to express yourself authentically and not be in fear of judgment, you can rest assured, you most likely have balanced throat chakra energy. However, if you find yourself fearful of speaking your soul's truth or cannot express yourself clearly or creatively, this is an indicator that your throat chakra is out of balance.

The throat chakra is connected with the thyroid gland. The thyroid is located in the throat and it is the largest organ in the endocrine system. The thyroid produces the hormones T4 and T3, which help maintain a normal blood pressure, heart rate, and muscle tone, as well as reproductive functions.

Balancing the Throat Chakra

In addition to meditating with a focus on the throat chakra, there are several other activities you can incorporate into your daily routine to help express and honor your authentic self.

1. Speak your truth and communicate clearly. The throat chakra is often blocked by the illusions we believe in, or in lies we tell ourselves and others, when we are ashamed about our authentic selves. When I first discovered how intuitive I was, I was terrified about what people would think. I had insight into what I was here to do, but I suppressed it and held it all in. This ultimately led to thyroid issues and my inability to live an authentic life for a long while. I knew how psychic I was but I was terrified to let others know. Slowly but surely, when strangers asked me what I did, I began to introduce myself as an intuitive healer. As time went on, it got easier.

Always tell others exactly how you are feeling. Even if you are feeling alone when you are communicating your feelings, communicate your truth. Often, because empaths are people pleasers and are scared to upset a person who is already at such a heightened level, they suppress what they truly want to say. This may be great for the other person, but not so great for an empath.

2. Sing or scream out loud. I don't care if you can sing or not—express yourself through music! If you are angry, sing it; sad, sing it; loving, sing it! One of my favorite activities when I am feeling a need to express myself or clear some energy is putting my earbuds in and singing loudly for hours. I feel empowered, authentic, and in tune. It also gives me the opportunity to lighten up and be silly if the moment arises. I also dance around like crazy when I am singing, which allows me another form of expression and provides me with a physical outlet to get the energy moving.

Don't be afraid to scream out loud—yes, you read that right. When the frustrations of life have you feeling like you cannot handle anymore, scream or seek some other type of physical release. It's a release that is much needed at times. There have been several points on my journey where I did not believe I could take on any more. I remember one evening, I drove myself out to an old field where I could stand alone and simply scream out loud where no one could hear me. I let it out, cried, and felt better shortly after. I simply needed the release because I was holding it all in.

3. Journal. Writing is a powerful tool. Another form of expression, write down everything you feel, think, and experience. For those of you who are drawn toward or know meditation is for you, a meditation journal is a powerful thing to have for referencing and wrapping your logical mind around what you experience during meditation.

4. Deep breathing. We take air in and out through the throat. We inhale freshness and let go of what is no longer needed. Deep breathing can help revitalize the thyroid gland by raising the body's vibration and life force energy.

Throat Chakra Affirmations

❖ I have a right to speak my truth

❖ I always speak directly from my heart

❖ I am authentic

❖ I allow open, clear, and honest communication into my life

❖ I communicate my feelings, no matter what

❖ I love to share my truth, wisdom, and experiences

❖ I know when it is time to listen

❖ I am peaceful

❖ I express myself with clarity and confidence

❖ I let go of the restraints that have held me back in the past

Third Eye Chakra

This vortex is associated with light, intuition, imagination, and clarity. If you know your purpose, honor and trust your intuition, and can meditate quite easily, you can rest assured, you most likely have balanced third eye chakra energy. However, if you find yourself doubting your intuition or cannot seem to trust yourself, your third eye chakra may be out of balance.

The third eye chakra is connected with the pineal gland. The pineal gland is a small endocrine gland in the brain that produces melatonin, a hormone that affects and balances sleep/wake patterns. Melatonin also affects our ability to adapt to change.

Balancing the Third Eye Chakra

In addition to meditating with a focus on the third eye chakra, there are several other activities you can incorporate into your daily routine to help heighten and trust your intuition.

1. Learn to see with your eyes closed. When you are relaxed and have your eyes closed or are getting ready to fall asleep, pay attention to what you see. Take note of the colors, shapes, images, animals, names, and visions that show up. Sometimes, the thing you see can almost show up like mini movie scenes. Trust that what you are seeing is valuable and being shown to you for a reason.

Doing this, you are tapping into your clairvoyance skills. Journal all that you see and then take time to look up the spiritual meaning to what you are seeing. Often, this is how we receive messages. This also helps us learn to understand what signs or symbols are for our own guidance and which are for guiding others.

2. Visualization exercises. Spend time every day visualizing or "daydreaming" about what you would like to manifest for you in the physical world. See it as if you already have it or are experiencing it. When I first knew I was to begin helping others through their awakening process, I had no idea how I was going to achieve this. However, I would sit down, close my eyes, and imagine talking to and helping people all over the world through the internet. Within a few months, this came into fruition for me.

3. Pay attention to your diet. Although sometimes this can be a little bit of a challenge for empaths (since we like to eat our feelings at times), it is essential to put high vibrational foods into your body, such as organic fruits and vegetables, and lessen the amount of processed foods you take in. In fact, as you begin to raise your vibration and your intuition becomes stronger, you may find yourself actually craving more high vibrational foods.

4. Keep a dream journal. We are more receptive to messages and guidance when we are asleep, which is a more natural and relaxed state. It is very important to keep a dream journal if you are receiving a lot of guidance this way. Even if the dream seems off the wall or way out of left field, I promise, there is a message in there for you. A lot of empaths will tap into past life memories or will literally receive a visit from a loved one or guide while asleep. As soon as you wake up, write down what you remember. This will open you up over time to really trust in what you are receiving. The more you trust, the more detailed guidance will be given.

5. Communicate with your spiritual team. Ask your team a question and then wait to see what appears in your mind's eye. This is a fun little exercise to practice, especially if you are a healer who is being guided to helping others. For example, ask, "What do I do next?" and see what appears. Write it down and then look it up.

Third Eye Chakra Affirmations

- ❖ I am connected to the divine
- ❖ I always honor and follow my intuition
- ❖ I know that it is safe for me to see truth
- ❖ I see
- ❖ My spiritual insight is clear

- ❖ I adapt to change gracefully
- ❖ I am intuitive
- ❖ I accept my path
- ❖ I am a calm and open clear channel
- ❖ I let the illusion of control go

Crown Chakra

This vortex is associated with spirituality, awareness, and connection to the divine. Often, it is referred to as a satellite or antennae that receives guidance from the higher realms. The crown chakra is the seat of cosmic consciousness.

If you are aware that you are a spiritual being having a physical experience, are connected to your divine wisdom, and feel very clear, you can rest assured, you most likely have a balanced energy. However, if you find yourself denying your spiritual connection, feeling misunderstood, or lacking understanding when it comes to who you truly are, your crown chakra may be out of balance.

The crown chakra is primarily connected with the pituitary gland, but it also works in harmony with the pineal gland and the hypothalamus. The pituitary gland and the hypothalamus work together to help regulate the endocrine system. Because of where the crown chakra is located, this chakra is connected with the brain and the entire nervous system.

Balancing the Crown Chakra

In addition to meditating with a focus on the crown chakra, there are several other activities you can incorporate into your daily routine to help with feeling a strong connection to the divine.

1. Allow yourself alone time. As an empath, it is essential to be able to connect to your own vibration. Empaths are so used to absorbing other people's thoughts, feelings, and energy that they can become unbalanced and can lose touch with who they are. Make time every day to be alone so you can connect to your internal guidance and gain clarity about who you truly are. During this time, reflect, practice gratitude, or pray—whatever resonates with you. Take a moment daily to connect with the divine.

2. Pay attention to and honor your recurring ideas. Recurring ideas often signify divine guidance, and you will have to check your logic at the door. I work with many empaths who are receiving the answers to their questions but are dismissing them as random thoughts or not logical. Your crown chakra is a direct link to the spirit, and spirit is not logical. Keep a notepad or something else nearby to jot down ideas that you have frequently.

3. Trust yourself. Trust in your inner wisdom and accept that not everything is logical or black and white. You are a spiritual being having a physical experience. Everything is happening in your life for a reason and it is important to have faith and trust that the guidance you are receiving is divine and accurate. Practicing faith every day is a powerful tool that will help strengthen your crown chakra.

4. Choose love. Align with the vibration of love. When you are living in the vibration of fear, you will not feel clear because it is impossible for love and fear to live in the same place. Align with what you feel is right. Drop the ego and let your beautiful heart win. No matter what you are being moved through in your life at any moment, choose to align with love. Love is hope, faith, and trust, full of infinite wisdom, while fear is worry, anxiety, or control. Fear stems from a lack of information. Ask yourself daily, "Am I choosing to align with love right now, or with fear?"

Crown Chakra Affirmations

❖ I am one with the divine

❖ I am light

❖ I am open to let go of my attachments

❖ I live in the present moment

❖ I know that all is well

❖ I have clarity

❖ I am whole

❖ I am an infinite being

❖ I know that I am divinely guided

❖ I am at peace

Foot Chakra

In addition to the seven main chakras discussed on the previous pages, I would like to mention how important it is to pay attention to the foot chakra. It is here that divine energy returns back to source. The foot chakra is very underrated and is often forgotten when it comes to healing. The foot chakra acts as a conduit for the divine energy we receive to pass through. The root chakra actually slows down the energy so it can be moved out through the feet. A healthy foot chakra helps energy pass to all of the chakras.

Since many empaths who will be reading this may be moving through an awakening, I want you to know that people who are being moved through the awakening process can experience extreme highs and extreme lows due to blocked energy in the feet. Many times, a blockage in the foot chakra happens when life gets to be too stressful or a bit much for them to handle. Here are some signs that your foot chakra is experiencing a block in energy flow:

◆ Suffering from insomnia

◆ Feelings of fatigue and tired often

◆ The feeling of not being grounded

◆ Anxiety or restlessness

- Feeling disconnected

- Feeling disoriented

> "*Chakra meditation is designed to bring you back to neutrality, to a place of balance. You might call this zero point, a place where you can begin again with a fresh, new mind.*" —Ilchi Lee

CHAPTER TEN

Tools for Empaths

It is essential for an empath to keep their energy clear so they can remain balanced and in tune with their own vibration. The following are tools that I personally recommend for clearing and grounding. Some of these tools you can use daily, like essential oils, while others, like reiki treatments, can be done weekly or monthly for energetic maintenance. In this chapter, you will learn about grounding tools, energy-clearing tools, and energy-balancing tools. You will also learn about tools to help you grow your psychic gifts.

The Importance of Being Grounded

In addition to the many challenges that come along with being an empath, one of the biggest challenges that I have personally experienced and have seen so many other empaths struggle with is not being grounded.

When one is properly grounded, they are energetically centered. Much like a tree that needs a strong root system in order to grow and remain stable, being grounded gives you a strong base and foundation to build on.

When you are not grounded, you suffer from energetic imbalances. It can feel as though your entire world is spinning out of control; it can literally feel as though you are out of your body. Every feeling you experience is based in fear and it is not a fun place to be.

Does this sound like something you have experienced? What was it like?

_____

_____

_____

_____

_____

Here are some other symptoms of being ungrounded:

◆ Feeling drained physically, mentally, emotionally, and spiritually. Your cup is empty, you are done.

◆ Being susceptible to surrounding energies; allowing the energy of other people to affect you more than normal.

◆ Inability to focus. You try but it doesn't matter what you do, you are feeling scattered and unable to do basic tasks or tackle projects that need to be tackled.

◆ Dizziness. You may feel you are spinning and need to lie down or sit just to rebalance.

◆ Your inner masculine/feminine energy is out of balance. If you have too much masculine energy, you may try to force an outcome and not let yourself go with the natural flow of life. If you have too much feminine, you may be swimming in the abyss of emotions and intuitive impressions without taking action toward what you desire.

◆ Feeling as if you are literally powerless; this comes with a weak solar plexus/power center.

◆ Inability to express yourself through creative endeavors or physically speaking up / expressing yourself.

- Consistently living in the future or the past; not allowing yourself to simply live in the moment.

- Holding onto physical things; having a hard time letting go in fear that you will not have enough. Highly materialistic.

- Highly skeptical, questioning things more than normal. Always feeling as though there has to be a logical or "rational" meaning for something. Having a hard time trusting your intuition or the synchronicities that are happening all around you.

- Suffering from inflammation that causes pain within your body.

The Science behind Grounding

According to Stephen Sinatra, M.D., the term grounding means to literally stick your bare feet on the ground. The reason this is beneficial for the human body is because the surface of the earth is full of negative electrons and the body absorbs these electrons through the bottom of the feet. Dr. Sinatra also believes that many of the chronic diseases that we suffer from come from inflammation, which is also linked to a lack of grounding. There are currently 21 published studies in the medical community on grounding and he expects more growth in this area.

> **"**In simple terms, what earthing does is literally quench the fires of inflammation. If inflammation is the source of all root illnesses and if you can impact inflammation, squelch it, and kill it, we are going to be healthier beings.**"** —Dr. Stephen Sinatra

Dr. Gaetan Chevalier, an engineer, believes that human beings become imbalanced when we do not receive enough of a negative charge.

He believes that we need grounding just as much as we need air, water, and sunshine.

Negative electrons are good for the human body because they help:

- promote a sense of calm

- neutralize free radicals

- promote a healthier sleep cycle

- balance the nervous system

- purify blood

- reduce inflammation

The human body is just a big piece of electrical equipment. We are bioelectrical beings, and just as electrical objects require grounding when they are placed anywhere to prevent surges or burnouts, so do we.

The benefits that grounding holds for empaths is obvious. It literally helps you rebalance and come back to your energy center. Many empaths have naturally done this since they were young. I have always gone barefoot outside as much as possible, even into adulthood. I never really knew why; I just knew that it simply felt better for me to walk around barefoot.

Follow these tips in addition to earthing to stay grounded:

Follow a healthful diet. Be mindful what you place into your body. Taking in low vibrational foods that are processed can cause anxiety. Eat foods that are whole and literally pulled from the ground, such as broccoli and carrots.

Drink enough water. Our bodies are made up of 75 percent water, so naturally, staying hydrated is very beneficial for energy and balance. Water helps to protect the energetic and physical body. Empaths need a lot of water. They will often crave it.

Practice yoga. Yoga is incredibly grounding. A lot of people will turn away from yoga because they feel it will be too much work, but yoga comes in all levels and works with the physical and energetic bodies to bring optimum balance. Yoga, in my opinion, serves everyone who tries it. For a wonderful grounding yoga exercise, see Breath of Fire Technique on page 120.

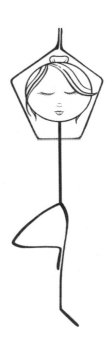

Step into your creativity. When we take a moment to step back from the chaotic world we live in and choose to be creative, this helps to make us feel better. It naturally causes us to live more in the moment because the creative project is the only thing we are focused on at that moment.

Smudge or sage. Smudging or saging yourself and your space helps to clear your energy field. If you are like many others and you find yourself not loving the smell of sage, use a sage room spray or burn Palo Santo instead.

Smudging or Saging

Smudging, sometimes known as saging, is the practice of burning plants (often, sage) to remove lower vibrational energy from people, spaces, or objects. As an empath, I have found this practice to be incredibly beneficial when it comes to clearing out energy that does not serve me. It is so easy and can be done quite quickly.

Smudging is not a new age practice; it has been used for centuries all over the world. Many countries and numerous religions use the art of burning herbs or oils to help purify surrounding spaces. When the space is clear of negative energy, an empath is more likely to feel more in balance.

In addition to providing energetic benefits, there has been a recent study published stating that burning sage has antiseptic benefits. The study titled "Medicinal Smokes," published by *The Journal of Ethnopharmacology*, claims that after a space has been saged, it reduces bacterial populations in the air by 94 percent.

How to Smudge Yourself

Start with an intention. Why are you saging yourself? Make it your intention to clear a specific energy.

Grab your smudge stick and light it on fire. A smudge stick is the bundle of plants that you will be burning, often including sage. Blow out the fire so the stick smokes, but does not burn. Make sure you have a window open while smudging to let fresh energy come into the area and negative energy leave.

To smudge, move the smudge stick near the part of the body that you wish to cleanse, directing the smoke in your direction. Start at your feet—I highly encourage you to do this barefoot so you can clear the foot chakras, but be careful not to burn yourself—and work your way up to over your head. Go down each of your arms as well. You can also create a smoke cloud and walk through it.

How to Smudge a Space

Start with an intention. Why are you feeling the need to sage your space? Make it your intention to clear a specific energy.

Grab your smudge stick, light it, and walk to all four corners of your space. Work your way up from the floor to the ceiling. Ask that all energy that is not of love and light be transmuted and cleared. Make sure you have windows open or a way for the energy that is not serving to leave.

After the room or space has been cleared, you can burn sweetgrass to call in the positive energy of the angelic realms, you can also ask for protection at this time if you would like. Sweetgrass does not burn the same way that sage does, so you will have to light it several times, but the scent and energy that it brings is totally worth it. If you do not want to deal with lighting the sweetgrass a few times, sweetgrass spray is also available.

How did you/your space feel before you cleared?

_____

_____

_____

_____

How do you/your space feel now?

_____

_____

_____

_____

Reiki and Empaths

At some point in their lives, many empaths will find themselves drawn toward energy healing, whether it is to receive healing or to become healers themselves. Reiki healing is a type of energy healing that is becoming very popular with the medical community. You can now find reiki being practiced in hundreds of hospitals across the United States. Dr. Mehmet Oz is one doctor who utilizes and understands the benefits of reiki masters/practitioners.

Reiki is an ancient art that treats the body, mind, and soul. It involves the practice of channeling life force energy through the physical and emotional body to help promote balance and an overall sense of wellbeing. It is important to note that reiki works in conjunction with and is not a replacement for regular medical or psychological treatment.

Reiki heals by allowing divine energy to flow through the chakras and the energy field surrounding the body, which can be affected due to negative thought patterns, trauma, emotional ailments, and more. Healing is possible because reiki raises the vibration of the person being treated. By healing our chakras, energy can flow more naturally, which helps the person being treated to heal and come back to a place of balance. If you have a hard time staying energetically balanced, feel emotionally or physically drained, or feel as though you are going through an awakening, it would be an ideal time to seek out a qualified reiki practitioner and receive a reiki treatment.

Reiki treatments are very relaxing and gentle. Some people experience a gentle tingling, and others experience stronger waves of energy or heat in certain areas. I have had clients on the table who seem to really notice the tingling above their head and through the bottom of their feet, but the tingling can really be felt anywhere.

Depending on what is there to heal or balance, an emotional release may be experienced as well. It is also very common to see flashes of color or receive messages/guidance from your team while on the reiki table.

> **"***As we get a better understanding of how little we know about the body, we begin to realize that the next big frontier in medicine is energy medicine. I think the most important alternative medicine secret is reiki.***"**
> —Dr. Mehmet Oz

Essential Oils

Essential oils are like little magic potions that have so many incredible benefits. They can help with physical and emotional ailments, and are a wonderful tool for keeping an empath in a state of balance. Essential oils have been utilized for their healing benefits for thousands of years and are known for their ability to promote an overall sense of wellbeing in an individual. I am so thankful for them and the role they have played on my journey.

Essential oils are made up of tiny plant molecules that are usually absorbed through the body and into the bloodstream or diffused to pass through the limbic system, which is located in the brain and helps us deal with and process emotions, memories, and stimulation.

When essential oils are used, they stimulate an action to heal the body or calm the mind. Essential oils can be and should be used daily, especially if you are trying to heal something in particular or if you are working toward a certain goal.

Essential Oils and Chakras

Essential oils can be incredibly helpful for balancing the chakras. Below are oil suggestions to use for balancing each of the eight chakras discussed in this book. There are several essential oil brands you can use. Young Living, Doterra, and NOW are a few of my favorites.

Root Chakra: frankincense, myrrh, sandalwood, cedarwood, vetiver

Sacral Chakra: orange, rose, jasmine, ylang ylang, cedarwood

Solar Plexus Chakra: bergamot, vetiver, frankincense, jasmine, sandalwood

Heart Chakra: rose, Joy by Young Living, lemongrass, jasmine, geranium

Throat Chakra: chamomile, basil, peppermint, sage, myrrh

Third Eye Chakra: Awaken by Young Living, sandalwood, frankincense, juniper, lavender

Crown Chakra: frankincense, myrrh, lavender, jasmine, Surrender by Young Living

Foot Chakra: rosewood, Grounding by Young Living, sandalwood, frankincense, myrhh

Using Crystals

Crystals are beautiful tools that can aid us during times of healing, soothing, or deeper awakening and enlightenment. They have always been regarded as a source of power, since ancient times. However, if you are a bit skeptical like I was when I was first introduced this concept, I totally understand. Many people find themselves wondering why rocks or stones would be beneficial to their healing. These beautiful gems are so much more than just colorful rocks, and there is a very valid reason aside from the spiritual aspect for people to carry and wear these stones.

Each of these stones vibrates at a different frequency. Think of them as tools that can help you tune your body instrument, like acupuncture without the needles. Since you are an energetic being, depending on what your needs are, you will find yourself drawn or attracted to different stones at certain points of your journey.

You may find yourself desiring to carry around or wear a certain stone daily. These stones can be worn or held during meditation, whatever feels right for you. Not only will you love the way they feel, but simply looking down at or knowing your crystals are with you will consciously remind you of what you are working on internally.

Below you will find a few essential crystals that I recommend all empaths have in their crystal collection. These are practical tools to help an empath with energy resets and balancing.

Amethyst. Amethyst is an incredible calming stone, which is good for an empath. Empaths thrive in calm environments. Amethysts are also excellent stones for increasing intuition. Associated with the third eye and crown chakras, this crystal will allow the empath to learn how to trust in their own intuition, an important lesson for empaths. It will also help empaths recognize their gifts and discern what is theirs and what is not.

Mugglestone/tiger iron. I giggled the first time I heard the name of this stone. It came through to me during a meditation session so I immediately thought about Harry Potter and had to check to see if there really was such a stone; of course there was. (Just another lesson for me in the beginning not to doubt what I was seeing during meditation!) Mugglestone, which contains hematite, is amazing for grounding and for those who tend to get extremely fatigued after being around others. It helps calm scattered energy and is associated with the lower chakras, root, sacral, and solar plexus chakras.

Rose quartz. Rose quartz is another stone that is incredibly calming. This was one of the first stones I began to work with. It is the stone of Mother Mary and is associated with the heart chakra and unconditional love. Since learning how to love and accept and honor your own heart is a crucial lesson for the empath, this stone is on my list of top stones that are essential for empaths.

Blue quartz. Blue quartz is a stress-relieving stone. It assists in calming an overactive mind, inspiring hope, and alleviating fear. This stone is associated with the throat chakra and can help aid with organization and self-discipline.

Obsidian. I honestly do not know what I would do without my obsidian. I own a very large piece and at times, I have sat it on my chest or held it in my palm during meditation just to ground myself well. Along with mugglestone, obsidian is one of my first go-to stones when I need some serious grounding and feel overwhelmed. Associated with the root chakra, this stone helps alleviate fear and will help the empath feel stable during times of overwhelm.

Sulfer cluster. Sulfer is an amazing tool for absorbing and transforming negative energy. It is a wonderful crystal to use when working on the solar plexus for self-confidence and will power.

Carnelian. Carnelian is a powerful crystal to use when you are ready to create something new and "take the leap," so to speak. This crystal is associated with the sacral chakra and helps you trust your intuition and create based on your intuitive impressions.

Moldavite. Referred to as "the holy grail" of stones, moldavite is an extremely high vibrational stone that can help bring about fast change in your life. Moldavite formed between 11 and 15 million years ago when a meteorite hit the earth's surface. Many star seeds are incredibly drawn to this stone; and it often enhances their meditations deeply. (Star seeds are advanced souls who have a mission to help assist earth ascend; these souls have an incredible amount of wisdom held within them that helps them be of service to mankind.) It is important to know that not everyone can handle the vibration of this stone. Some find it to be too much and have reported nausea or a spinning feeling. Also, if you decide to add this beautiful crystal to your collection, make sure you are purchasing an authentic moldavite.

Clear Quartz. Clear quartz is known as an amplifier and is considered to be a stone of power. This is an excellent crystal to hold when placing intentions or when manifesting and aligning with a goal.

Selenite. Associated with the angelic realms, selenite helps dispel negative energy and can assist with clearing all of the chakras. It can assist with opening up the higher chakras. This is a wonderful crystal to work with when it comes to any type of spiritual work.

Blue lace agate. Associated with the throat chakra, blue lace agate helps you speak your truth, and it is also considered to be a protection stone for many healers. I personally wore this stone around my neck every day for about a year when I was trying to be brave enough to embrace my gifts and discuss awakenings on a very public level. It's a powerful stone and will always hold a special place in my heart. This is a fantastic stone to have for those who need to calm an overactive mind.

Selecting the Right Crystal

When selecting your crystal, you will find that most times, you will naturally be drawn to the exact crystal that you need for that very moment in your life. Your energetic body will be attracted to the energy that it desires for tuning and balancing. When it comes to knowing if you have selected the right crystal, hold the crystal you feel drawn to in your left hand and take a moment to tune in and really feel the energy emerging from the stone. If it is the stone for you, you will often feel little tingles in your palm when you are holding it. This can almost feel like ants are crawling around on your palm. This is usually similar to the feeling many healers experience when they meditate or are performing reiki healing on another.

It is important to note that just because a crystal is beautiful, this does not mean that this is the stone you need. Crystal tool selection is never about what looks prettier. There will be times when something plain and not so enticing will end up being the most perfect stone for you.

Caring for Your Crystals

Crystals pick up and absorb energy from anyone who handles them and it is essential to keep them clean. There are a few ways you can do this:

◆ Sage your crystals.

◆ Run your crystals under water or let them soak in Epsom salt water. Make sure this method is only used on crystals that can get wet; not all crystals should get wet, like selenite.

◆ Place your crystals outside and let the sun or moon charge them. New moons and full moons are a perfect time for this.

◆ Infuse your crystals with reiki energy and symbols.

◆ Use selenite to clean your other crystals. Selenite has cleansing properties, and you can even purchase a selenite pad to keep your crystals on.

> **"***In a crystal we have the clear evidence of the existence of a formative life-principle, and though we cannot understand the life of a crystal, it is nonetheless a living being.***"** —Nikola Tesla

Angel or Oracle Cards

Oracle and angel cards are some of the best tools to help an empath. It's important to remember that these cards are simply a tool to help you open up and that the "magic" is truly inside of you. The cards are there to act as a catalyst in some way to help you learn to trust, to open you up to realizing that there is more to this world than we usually allow ourselves to perceive.

When divine intervention happened in my life and synchronicity was getting my attention in ways I had never experienced, I found myself intuitively picking up oracle and angel cards. My rational and analytical mind was fascinated by the very practical messages that seemed to come out in the cards and how in sync those messages were with where I was in my journey. The more I explored this tool, the more I began to allow everything that I was feeling inside to come through. The more I allowed myself to trust in what I was feeling while playing with them, the more clarity came from within, and that same clarity would come out in the cards.

Eventually, I began to trust more. I stopped doubting and my intuitive gifts began to expand. My clair gifts grew stronger and the chapters in my life began to make total sense.

Remember that if you choose to use oracle cards or other divination tools, you should aim not to become emotionally attached to the outcome. When you have an emotional attachment to the outcome (which you naturally will when reading yourself), the reading will come out jumbled or you may simply walk away more frustrated and confused than when you first started. Be open to all types of answers.

One of the most common things empaths have to learn is that they will not be able to read themselves or know certain things about themselves, even if they may have total clarity when it comes to another's journey. Just because an empath has beautiful intuitive and psychic gifts does not mean the empath will know everything that is coming up for them. Just like every other soul enrolled on this planet, an intuitive empath will have their own lessons to be moved through. Often, one of the first crucial lessons an intuitive empath will have to learn is how to trust in themselves and their own intuition and inner voice.

These cards exist to help remind you that you hold all of the wisdom you need inside of you, and that wisdom is held within your heart. You do not need this tool to connect with spirit or God, but if you feel like you would like to open yourself up more and learn to trust in your infinite wisdom, they are an amazing gift, and I am personally very thankful for them.

Love Who You Are

Take a chance and challenge yourself to unlearn everything you ever thought you knew. Surrender and know that you have the gifts and beautiful ability to feel so deeply for a purpose. From here it is about trusting your heart and releasing anything that is not in alignment with what you truly are, love.

Know that every situation you have ever been exposed to has served a purpose; whether negative or positive, you were learning from this moment and those yet to come. Earth is a school. The chapters of your life are beginning to make sense. Surrender to the process and trust in your soul's journey.

Remember this: You are awakening. It's a process and cannot be rushed. You are an old soul here for a divine purpose and your light is needed. You had to experience everything you have from childhood through today so you could level up and build a nice solid foundation for yourself based on the truth within your heart. Keep listening and know that you are your own guru. The time to take back your power is now. You are not a victim. You are the magician.

Acknowledgments

Thank you to every soulmate of mine who has caused me growth. To those of you who have shown me love, thank you. To those of you who have shown me fear, thank you. To those of you who have shown me *me*, thank you.

To my family, I love you all so much. You've slowly witnessed me return to my heart space over the years and encouraged me to grow more. I appreciate all of your love and nurturing. Thank you for accepting me for me and pushing me to keep going. Mom, Craig, Jason, Nichole, and Jaime: I love you. Bryan and Lauren, you are in my heart and thoughts daily.

Leah: You know every reason why you are here. You believed in me long before I did. You are the true definition of a friend. Always there, never judging, and allowing me to speak my own truth. Thank you for the encouragement and all the subtle pushes forward. I love you.

Alisha: You haven't left my side once. Your continued support continues to baffle me at times. Your heart is pure and I am forever grateful for you. No matter how many times I have needed you, you've always been there for me... through all the feels. I love you.

Lanny: Thank you for allowing me the space I needed to grow. This book would've been a lot harder to write if I didn't have the space I needed to discover and remember who and what I am. Trixie and I love you very much.

Becky: Thank you for helping me navigate through all of the energy and shifts. You have truly helped me understand myself and my gifts again and again. Thank you for believing in me, encouraging me, and holding space for me as I grow. You are the one person in this world who has ever truly understood my entire journey. My heart loves you so much.

Lexy: There are no words. You've loved me, accepted me, trusted me, and believed in me from the moment I spoke to you about what I was experiencing years ago. My soul bestie. Forever. I love you.

Cathy: I often refer to you as my Mr. Miyagi. Words cannot express. I love you. A true teacher and healer. Thank you for the continued perspective shifts.

Delia: The silliest of souls we are. Thank you for allowing me to just be me. Soul sisters. My girl. Always.

Shane: You always listen. You always support. I love you.

David: "Those who bare the brightest lights have the most stones thrown at them." I finally understand this statement. Earth is a school. It was about trusting my inner voice all this time. Thank you.

Deborah and Michael: The invaluable lessons and insights the two of you provided me stay with me every day. True healers and I feel so blessed to have met you both. You held space for me during a time in my life when I needed it most. You saw me. Thank you.

Ulysses Press: Thank you for the opportunity that you provided me. I am honored. I've told my family and friends for years that I always felt like I had a book in me, and as it turns out… I did.

About the Author

Stephanie Jameson is an intuitive psychic empath and certified reiki master. Although she is gifted with all clairs, her strongest clairs are clairvoyance and clairaudience. She works with individuals all over the world who find themselves being moved through an awakening/ascension journey, some who are discovering that they themselves may also have light-working gifts to share. She understands that the separation from others and from spirit is just an illusion. She also understands the struggles that come along with being an energetically sensitive person. A lesson that many healers need to learn, she knows that she was moved through these experiences firsthand so she could ultimately help others recognize their own gifts and trust in themselves. Nothing brings Stephanie more joy than helping others find peace, clarity, and healing. Stephanie currently resides in Boise, Idaho. Visit Stephanie's website at www.divinesouljourney.net.